A Guide to the New Language of Accounting and Finance

A Guide to the New Language of Accounting and Finance

Roger Hussey and Audra Ong

BUSINESS EXPERT PRESS

Leader in applied, concise business books

A Guide to the New Language of Accounting and Finance

Cover design by Charlene Kronstedt

Interior design by Exeter Premedia Services Private Ltd., Chennai, India

First published in 2021 by
Business Expert Press, LLC
222 East 46th Street, New York, NY 10017
www.businessexpertpress.com

ISBN-13: 978-1-63742-129-1 (paperback)
ISBN-13: 978-1-63742-130-7 (e-book)

Business Expert Press Financial Accounting and Auditing Collection

Collection ISSN: 2151-2795 (print)
Collection ISSN: 2151-2817 (electronic)

First edition: 2021

10 9 8 7 6 5 4 3 2 1

Description

The disciplines of accounting and finance have been rapidly changing in recent years. The methods and techniques now being used have created a new language for managers, students, practitioners, academics, and all those who are connected in some way with business and investment activities. To understand and work within an environment that is in a constant state of flux can be challenging, and this book provides a resource of information and guidance.

The *Guide* focusses specifically on the terms used in accounting and finance. Important terms and phrases are identified but with a much longer, in-depth explanation than you would normally find in a dictionary. Not only does each entry give a thorough explanation of each term, but most entries also provide two or more references to academic articles that go into much greater depth. Hence, the entries give the reader immediate access to the literature.

The *Guide* also comments on the contribution of the articles that adds to our knowledge. This approach allows the reader to obtain a much deeper level of understanding much more quickly than is available from the usual dictionary. At the end of the book, the full reference to all the articles that have been cited in the text is given including a list of the many acronyms used in the world of accounting and finance.

The *Guide* includes both U.S. and International Financial Reporting and accounting practices and regulations. This means that there are some language differences particularly with the terms *share* (International) and *stock* (U.S.), and *checks* (U.S.) and *cheques* (International). The *Guide* draws the reader's attention to these differences where they occur.

Keywords

accounting rate of return; capital reduction; harvesting strategy; kaizen costing; non fungible tokens; sustainability accounting; Z-score

Preface

This book is not a dictionary of accounting and finance terms, but a comprehensive guide to the various aspects of the subjects. A brief explanation is given for each of the selected terms, and most entries provide references to academic articles that go into much greater depth, thus giving the reader immediate access to the literature. This approach allows the reader to obtain a much deeper level of understanding more quickly than is available from a dictionary. At the end of the book, the full reference to cited articles is given plus a list of acronyms.

The *Guide* includes both U.S. and International Financial Reporting and accounting practices and regulations. This means that there are some language differences particularly with the terms *share* (International) and *stock* (U.S.), and *checks* (U.S.) and *cheques* (International). The explanations are such that this should not cause any problems to the reader.

A

Absorption Costing, also known as full costing, is the method used by some companies to identify the total material and labor costs incurred in providing a service or a product and the amount would also include overhead costs such as administration, distribution, and sales costs. These additional costs, such as administration, are usually attributed to the accounting period in which the costs are incurred. Although absorption costing is normal in manufacturing companies, it is also used in other sectors. As some costs, such as administration, are fixed for a period irrespective of the amount of activity, the calculated cost per unit will fluctuate from one accounting period to another depending on the level of activity. A product that seemed profitable in one accounting period when production was high could be unprofitable in another period with a decline in production. Some would contend that activity-based costing is a preferable method for overcoming this issue (Omar and Tang 2019) although it is frequently used. A survey (Laing and Perrin 2018) conducted in the Australian printing industry found that absorption costing was the predominant method.

Accounting Concepts: See Conceptual Framework.

Accounting Equation is the formula that supports the use of the double-entry system of accounting. It reflects the structure of a balance sheet and is calculated as Assets = Liabilities + Capital. Assets are a company's resources and liabilities are a company's obligations being the amounts the company owes. The owners' capital or stockholders' capital (also referred to as equity) is the amount left over after liabilities are deducted from assets. An increase or decrease in total assets must be reflected by an equal increase or decrease in liabilities and capital, thus the balance sheet will always balance. The accounting equation is based on an entity view of a business. A propriety view would deduct liabilities from assets to calculate the capital, that is the owners' financial interest in the business. Although an apparently simple equation, any accounting professor will confirm that students find it very difficult to understand and Phillips and Heiser (2011) researched accounting equation and addressed this issue.

Accounting Rate of Return (ARR) is a ratio that measures the financial performance of an organization for a defined period by expressing profits as a percentage of capital employed. The ratio may take profit after or before interest and taxation. The method focuses on net operating income as calculated under accounting procedures and does not relate to cash flows. The ARR is also used by some organizations to assess the return generated from a capital investment. The ARR is a percentage return and it does not identify the time value of money or risks for long-term investments. A useful review of the literature on accounting-based estimates of the expected rate of return on equity (capital) is given by Easton and Monahan (2016).

Accounting Standards Advisory Forum (ASAF) was established in 2013 and supports the International Financial Reporting Standards Foundation in developing globally accepted high-quality accounting standards. It has 12 members from different geographic regions and a nonvoting chair. It meets four times a year for two days, normally in London, UK. It was established to contribute toward the development, in the public interest, of a single set of high-quality understandable, enforceable, and globally accepted Financial Standards to serve investors and other market participants in making informed resource allocations and other economic decisions. The background to the development of international standard regulations is given the comprehensive book Aiming for Global Accounting Standards: The International Accounting Standards Board, 2001–2011 by Camfferman and Zeff (2015). The website of the ASAF is www.ifrs.org/groups/accounting-standards-advisory-forum.

Accounting Standards Board (ASB) There are several ASBs, and it is preferable that you identify the particular one in which you are interested. The main ones are the Financial Accounting Standards Board (FASB) in the United States and the International Accounting Standards Board. The purpose of all the Accounting Boards is to establish the practices and procedures used by companies and auditors in relation to the financial statements issued by companies.

Accounting Standards Codifications (ASCs) are issued by the FASB in the United States. They are effective for interim and annual periods ending after September 15, 2009. All existing accounting standards documents are superseded by the ASC. The codification has organized the thousands of GAAP pronouncements and all other accounting literature not included in the Codification is now deemed nonauthoritative. Toemer (2009) provides a guide to using the codifications https and further information can be found on //asc.fasb.org/.

Accounting Standards Updates (ASUs) are issued by the FASB and are also issued for amendments to the SEC content in the FASB codification, as well as for editorial changes. These updates are important and comment on their impact on financial reporting is prominent in the accounting press. For comment on individual ASUs, see the articles by Rottkamp (2019) Carey and Dyson (2017). Information on the ASUs issued can be found from the FASB website at the following link: www.fasb.org/jsp/FASB/Page/SectionPage&cid=1218220137102.

Activity Based Costing (ABC) was proposed as an alternative to full costing by Kaplan and Bruns (1987). They demonstrated the value of the technique in the manufacturing sector where the proportion of the direct costs is falling and that of the indirect costs is increasing in importance. Since that date, the use of the technique has spread with adherents in both the manufacturing and service sectors. It is impossible to assess the extent of usage of ABC by companies. Dugdale and Jones (1997) conducted a telephone survey in the UK and concluded that evidence from a prior questionnaire study overestimated the extent of usage. This was because the responses to the questionnaire were either mistaken, prone to exaggeration, or ambiguous. This conclusion was confirmed in a later study (White, Anitsal, and Anitsal 2015), which referred to the ABC Paradox. The findings showed that although adoption of ABC was developing in foreign nations and in some American and European business sectors, there is a gap between the claims made on behalf of the method and the actual rate of adoption. One potential answer to the question, the answer to identifying the rate of adoption of ABC, is that companies devise, structure, and implement a costing system to meet their own particular strategic needs. Rankin (2020) noted that the results of his research study in the United States showed that three variables were found to be negatively associated with ABC adoption: cost structure, intensity of completion, and industry sector.

Activity Based Management is closely related to Activity Based Costing and also concentrates on corporate activities (Căpușneanu and Martinescu 2010). Organizations undertake activities that consume resources. If these activities are analyzed and monitored, costs can be controlled at source. For instance, some activities can be enhanced and some may be eliminated. The activity is deemed value-added if the customer is willing to pay for it. Nonvalue adding activities should be eliminated if this would not affect the customer's perceived value of the product/service or impair the function and operation of the organization. A very thoughtful summary of the literature and an original research project argues that it is the stage of development of an organization that is crucial in ascertaining the appropriateness of ABM practices (Phan, Baird, and Blair 2014).

Adaptive Expectation Hypothesis is a theory to predict interest rates based on the assumption that future movements in variables can be determined by an analysis of past patterns. Much of the literature on the subject dates from the 1980s, but a later study by Chetan (2011) on the nature of expectations formed by manufacturing plants as they plan their own capital expenditures concluded that both conventional rational expectations and adaptive expectations hypotheses are inconsistent with the data, which instead favors a regressive expectations formation process. A more recent research by Caporalea and Plastun (2019) examined the price overreactions in the U.S. stock market by focusing on the Dow Jones Industrial Index over the period 1990 to 2017. The results showed that the frequency of overreactions varies over time and is consistent with the Adaptive Expectations Hypothesis.

Adverse Audit Opinion is when an auditor makes a statement in their audit report that the financial statements do not meet the standards required. Such a situation can arise when the auditor considers that the financial statements are misleading. The existing literature suggests that internal control weaknesses are associated with impaired financial reporting quality and the possibility of financial statement frauds. Thus, these disclosures of weakness should be viewed as bad news by market participants. Research by Shelton and Whittington (2008) focusing on investment concluded that adverse audit opinion on the effectiveness of internal control results in investment analysts making a higher assessment of company risk, a lower assessment of the strength of internal control over financial reporting, and a marginally significant difference in the likelihood of recommending stock to their client. A more recent U.S. study by Adhikari, Guragai, and Seetharaman (2020) suggests that investors' perceptions regarding audited weakness disclosures have become more prevalent in recent years.

Algorithm is a set of instructions or rules for a process to be followed, particularly by a computer, in calculations or other problem-solving operations. The instructions may be simple, for example, multiplying two numbers, or can be complex programming. Algorithms are often created as functions. Chilakapati and Rochford (2020) suggested that there are two methods in developing the instructions. One is a Decision Tree that use a branch-like model of binary decisions that lead to possible outcomes. This method is frequently used within corporate finance functions. The second method is a Random Forest Regressor that uses subsets of data to build numerous smaller decision trees. The results of these are aggregated to arrive at a prediction or classification. There is a substantial number of academic articles focusing on algorithms, and one recent article specific to accounting is by Yao, Guarda, Lopes, and Rocha (2019).

Alternative Performance Measures (APM): See Key Performance Indicators (KPIs).

Altman's Z-Score: See Corporate Failure Prediction.

American Institute of Certified Professional Accountants was founded in 1887 and provides technical advice and guidance to its members. This includes developing technical and behavioral standards and guidance; establishing training: development, monitoring, and enforcement processes to help ensure that those standards are applied; and promoting thought leadership programs. The behavioral standards are usually referred to as codes of ethics or of professional conduct, and these codes usually refer to the profession's public interest obligation. The nature of the public role of accountants is discussed in an article by Bromwell (2017). The informative website of AICPA is www.aicpa.org/about.html.

Amortization is normally considered to be charging the initial cost of an asset over its expected useful working life to the Income Statement. In these instances, the term that is also used frequently is depreciation. However, the term amortization is sometimes used for the action of paying off debt over time in regular installments of interest and principal, for example, mortgage amortization (Saibeni 2018). From a conceptual point of view, there are few issues, but problems can arise. FASB sought comments on accounting for "Identifiable Intangible Assets and Subsequent Accounting for Goodwill." It required input on whether the benefits of the current goodwill impairment accounting model justify the cost to prepare and audit the information for public business entities, and if not, whether some form of goodwill amortization should be considered. The issue was explored by Betancourt and Irving (2019) who suggest that amortization of goodwill would lead to a decline in companies' earnings and earnings-based financial ratios. They argue that any move in this direction would likely meet intense and critical comment and debate from preparers, users, and auditors. The appropriate accounting treatment of goodwill has always been a subject of debate and whether amortization is appropriate is still undecided. FASB has updated their project statement "Identifiable Intangible Assets and Subsequent Accounting for Goodwill," and the most recent update can be found on www.fasb.org/jsp/FASB/FASBContent_C/ProjectUpdateExpandPage&cid=1176171566054

Analysis of Variances is a much-used statistical test that involve two or more groups. The results indicate whether survey or experiment results are significant or whether the null hypothesis should be accepted to the alternate hypothesis. There are many articles on this topic covering different industries and various countries. Unless you have a strong statistical background, you will find that most of the literature requires substantial thought.

Analytics is a term that usually appears in a research study that is concerned with understanding phenomena by discovering and measuring causal relationships. Increasingly, the techniques and processes of data analytics have been developed into mechanical processes and algorithms that work over raw data for human consumption. It has been argued that business analytics has been strongly influenced by the changes and innovations in the sphere of information communications technologies. One influence has been the emergence of Big Data, and the other is the increasing business need for data and analytics democratization (Soldić-Aleksić, Chroneos-Krasavac, and Karamata 2020).

Annual Percentage Rate (APR) is a calculation that measures the interest charges on a loan as a percentage of the loan amount outstanding. The application of this method and the publication of the rate is an attempt to ensure that borrowers can compare the true cost of credit from different lenders. APR contrasts with the flat rate method that can be misleading since it shows an interest charge that is lower than the effective rate. Several researchers have considered various aspects of interest on loans and one sphere is the loans taken on payday by employees. There is a concern that such lenders suffer from high APRs, misleading or inaccurate information, and a continuous circle of debt, and Kubálek, Fišerová, and Paseková (2019) considered debtor behavior and the relationship between debt expenses and insolvency. Bronson and Smith (2017), however, argued from research conducted in Southeast Alabama that high APRs represent the costs of lending to a financially risky population, not exorbitant profits and that many proposed regulations would not be effective.

Annuity is an amount paid out every year to an individual, usually a retiree. The money normally comes from an insurance policy. It can be split up into smaller amounts and paid out more frequently, such as monthly. It is usually paid for the rest of the beneficiary's life. Although the topic may not be of general interest, Tricker (2018) raises the interesting question whether a rational individual who owns an annuity should invest more in his or her longevity in order to receive more payments and thereby extend his or her life expectancy and contends that there is a growing body of empirical evidence supporting it.

Arbitrage is a method for making a profit as a result of a price differential in different markets. It involves the purchase and subsequent sale of such items as commodities, stock, and derivatives. An example would be the purchase of stock (shares) listed on the UK Stock Exchange and simultaneously selling the same stock on the National Association of

Securities Dealers Automated Quotation (NASDAQ) if the net selling price on NASDAQ is slightly higher than the net buying price on the UK Stock Exchange. Currency exchange differences would also need to be recognized in the calculations. Arbitrage can be incorrectly defined (Moosa 2010), but the topic receives considerable academic interest; Jarrow and Protter (2013) addressed arbitrage costs in the G7 stock market.

Artificial Intelligence (AI) has been defined as "a system's ability to interpret external data correctly, to learn from such data, and to use those learnings to achieve specific goals and tasks through flexible adaptation" (Kaplan and Haenlein 2019). There are different types of AI with general AI that refers to computer software that can think and act on its own; nothing like this currently exists and narrow AI that refers to computer software that relies on highly sophisticated, algorithmic techniques to find patterns in data and make predictions about the future. In this sense, the software "learns" from existing data and hence is sometimes referred to as "machine learning" but this should not be confused with actual learning (Raj and Seamans 2019). It is argued that when AI reaches mainstream usage, it may no longer be considered as "artificial." Some may discount the behavior of an AI program by arguing that it is not real intelligence and the task could be resolved by a human.

Asset Turnover Ratio measures a firm's ability to generate sales from its asset base. It is calculated by dividing the net sales by the total assets. The reasoning is that an organization must produce income from its net assets otherwise they are a drain on its resources or efficiency. A study by Patin, Rahman, and Mustafa (2020) concluded that to increase total asset turnover ratios, a company should effectively utilize physical infrastructure to generate additional income, adopt just-in-time approach to manage inventory, lessen use of assets to generate certain level of profitable sales, expedite collection of accounts receivables, and ensure capital discipline.

Association of Chartered Certified Accountants (ACCA) was founded in the UK in 1904 and has a membership of almost 230,000 with a much larger number studying for its examinations and it has a strong presence internationally. The term "Chartered" in ACCA qualification refers to the Royal Charter granted in 1974. Chartered Certified Accountant is a legally protected term. Individuals who describe themselves as Chartered

Certified Accountants must be members of ACCA, and if they carry out public practice engagements, they must comply with additional regulations such as holding a practicing certificate, carrying liability insurance, and submitting to inspections. The Association of Authorized Public Accountants (AAPA), one of the British professional bodies for public accountants, has been a subsidiary of ACCA since 1996.

Association of Collegiate Schools of Business (ACSB) was founded initially in 1916. Its name was changed to the American Association of Collegiate Schools of Business (AACSB) in 1925, and in that year, it established a permanent standing Committee on Business Research. Its mission is to foster engagement, accelerate innovation, and amplify impact in business education. It is a main source for data and statistics on business schools, both online and through its printed publications. Their website is www.aacsb.edu/contact.

Association of International Accountants (AIA) was founded in 1928 and is a global membership body for professional accountants. It is a Recognized Qualifying Body (RQB) for statutory auditors in the UK and regulated by the Financial Reporting Council (FRC). AIA is a Prescribed Body under the Companies (Auditing and Accounting) Act 2014 in the Republic of Ireland. AIA is a supervisory body under the UK Money Laundering Regulations and is a Commonwealth Accredited Organization.

Audit Expectation Gap is usually regarded as the difference between auditors' opinion of their duties and the expectations of the users of the financial information. One reason for the gap may be that public expectations are higher than the actual performance required of the auditor. For example, the users of financial information may believe that auditors will detect all fraud and misdemeanors of any size that is not the case. Another aspect to the divide may be that the users' opinions are reasonable but the auditor does not satisfy them. This failure on the auditors' part may lead to high-profile financial scandals. The expectation gap is not only applicable in the United States and United Kingdom, and there are numerous articles based on research in different countries. These usually generate useful advice and a recent example is a study of the position in Jordan (Toumeh, Sofri, and Siam 2018). There are much fewer articles giving the auditor's perspective, but Peterson (2016) provides such a view with sound suggestions as to improvements that could be made in the audit process. A very strongly referenced article by Bleibtreu and Stefani (2018) includes aspects of auditing regulations in the United Kingdom and United States and examines in detail the discussions on mandatory audit firms' rotations.

Audit Opinion is a certification by the auditors that records whether material misstatements exist in the financial statements that have been examined. The auditor's opinion accompanying a company's financial statement usually concludes that they are presented fairly in all materials respects in accordance with existing regulations. The auditor's report is addressed to the shareholders but the question arises whether the auditors' involvement with a company and close contact they have with directors, which is necessary to conduct their work, threatens their independence. Auditors are required to state whether they have significant doubt about their client's ability to continue as a going concern. This is known as the going concern opinion (GCO) and has attracted considerable research attention. The important role of auditors has attracted several research studies that cover many topics. A well-referenced study by Berglund, Herrmann, and Lawson (2018) examined managerial ability to influence the accuracy of auditors' going concern information signal. Hardies, Breesch, and Branson (2016) concluded from their research of financially distressed Belgian companies that female auditors produce higher audit quality. Even the timing of the appointment of auditors can have consequences, and Pacheco-Paredes, Rama, and Wheatley (2017) identified the following: (1) auditor changes closer to the year-end are associated with longer reporting lags and lower audit quality; (2) both audit fees and audit report lags are higher when there is a hiring lag between announcements of the predecessor auditor's dismissal and the hiring of the successor auditor; and (3) the appointment of new executives is associated with the timing of the auditor change, suggesting that client executives have a significant role in the auditor-hiring process.

Auditing Standards set out the procedures that accountants should follow when conducting an audit of financial statements. The organizations that regulate all aspects of the auditing of financial statements have very useful websites. In the United States, Generally Accepted Accounting Principles (GAAP) refer to a common set of accounting principles, standards, and procedures issued by the FASB (www.fasb.org/home). Public companies in the United States must follow GAAP when their accountants compile their financial statements. The Financial Reporting Council (FRC) is an independent regulator in the United Kingdom and Ireland and responsible for regulating auditors, accountants, and actuaries and setting the UK's Corporate Governance and Stewardship Codes. Their website is www.frc.org.uk/. International Standards on Auditing (ISA) are professional standards for the auditing of financial information. These standards are issued by the International Federation of Accountants (IFAC). The website is www.iaasb.org/. These standards do not override a specific country's regulations governing the audit of financial statements. Although the various boards have the direct responsibility, accounting professionals and interested government departments would make their opinions well known to the standards setting bodies. It is argued that auditing standards may restrict auditors' exercise of professional judgment resulting in compliance with the standard but reducing auditors' incentives to become competent in the first place (Gao and Zhang 2019). A substantial amount of academic audit research is conducted but it can be argued that the findings are not systematically and effectively transferred to auditing policy makers.

B

Balance Sheet, sometimes referred to as the equity statement or statement of financial position, shows the totals of a company's assets, liabilities, and shareholders' equity at a particular date. It is one of the three financial statements used to evaluate a business; the other two are the cash flow statement and the income statement. Edwards (2014) described the development of the balance sheet and its history. The mathematics of the balance sheet equation Assets (A) – Liabilities (L) = Capital (C) has become a foundation for teaching bookkeeping and was devised in 1494 by Pacioli's Summa de Arithmetica Geometria Proportioni et Proportionalita (Sangster and Scataglinibelghitar 2010). FASB is attempting to improve guidance used to determine whether debt should be classified as a current or noncurrent liability on a statement of financial position. The board issued its first proposal on the issue in January 2017. The initial proposal contained provisions to replace the current, fact-specific guidance with an overarching, cohesive principle for determining whether debt or other instruments within the scope of the proposal should be classified as a current or noncurrent liability as at the date of the statement of financial position. Comments from stakeholders, including the Private Company Council, led FASB to issue added proposed requirements related to unused long-term financing arrangements, such as a line of credit and grace periods. The revised proposed Accounting Standards Update (ASU) seeks comments on these changes, as well as the expected costs and benefits of the proposed amendments (ASB 2018).

Balanced Scorecard provides a framework that allows managers to focus on both financial and nonfinancial measures to assess company performance. It is based on the proposition that the following four critical success factors or perspectives capture the strategy of an organization. These are financial, customer, internal business, and growth. The concept was developed by Kaplan and Norton, and there are several articles by them in the literature as well as a book. An early and useful article is "The

Balanced Scorecard—Measures That Drive Performance" by Kaplan and Norton (1992). More recent articles have looked at a wide spread of the use of the Balanced Scorecard and its possible enlargement to include multiple stakeholder goals thus becoming a "stakeholder scorecard." In a well-referenced article, Hansen and Schaltegger (2018) reviewed the different opinions and suggested the future developments.

Bank for International Settlements was originally established in 1930. Since 1986, it has acted as a clearing house for interbank transactions. BIS is owned by 63 central banks, representing countries from around the world that together account for about 95 percent of world GDP. Its head office is in Basel, Switzerland. Their helpful website is www.bis.org/about/index.htm

Basic Earnings Per Share is the earnings per share (EPS) calculated by dividing the amount of net profit attributable to ordinary shareholders for a financial period by the weighted average number of ordinary shares outstanding during the period. An article by Rashty (2012) explains the application in the United States of the two-class method in the calculation of basic and diluted earnings per share (EPS) for stock compensation awards that are considered participating securities under Accounting Standards Codification (ASC) 260.

Bear Market refers to a weak, sluggish stock market where prices and share volumes are decreasing. The opposite to this is a Bull Market. There is a considerable volume of research on market behavior, and "sell in May and go away" is still the strategy of some investors. Hirsch (2016) noted that since 1950, stock returns, as measured by the Dow Jones Industrial Average, have advanced by nearly 7.5 percent during the months from November to April but only 0.30 percent during the months from May to October. The May to October period, in particular, is highlighted by September's historically negative monthly return of 0.75 percent, the worst performing month for equities. Such patterns were first officially published in the Stock Trader's Almanac (Hirsch 1986). Not surprisingly, given the high correlations across equity market measures, the more-diversified S&P 500 posts an average of 1.14 percent from November to April compared with 0.25 percent from May to October. However, Mackey (2019) argued that the behavior of the financial markets is better understood by classifying them as bear, bull, wolf, and eagle environments.

Benchmarking has attracted numerous researches and articles. At its simplest, it can be defined as the process of comparing your business to similar businesses in your industry. However, it has expanded to cover a large range of diverse activities including the UK's decision to leave the common market (De Vries 2017) and technological innovation in health systems in Canada (Prada 2008).

Benefits Cost Ratio evaluates a proposed project or activity by comparing the potential benefits to the costs that will be incurred. Where the benefits exceed the costs, the proposal is financially attractive. The benefits may be enjoyed by some groups and the costs borne by others, and this makes any analysis more complex, especially if there are some nonfinancial factors to be taken into account. A study by Hess (2007) examined the success and failures of transparency programs in the United States. The research identified the key factors for ensuring the success of social reporting over the long term. These factors include increasing the benefits-to-costs ratios of both the users of the information and the disclosers. There seem to be no boundaries where the use of this ratio can be used, and Brent (2019) conducted an analysis of hearing aids, including the benefits of reducing the symptoms of dementia.

Big Data. It is now possible to capture very large volumes of data, both unstructured and structured, but this cannot be analyzed effectively with traditional methods. The problem is finding the best method to analyze this data to assist improved decision making. There are several examples of the analysis of Big Data and these are usually specific to the issues in a particular industry or situation. A useful review of the literature and an explanation of the mechanisms through which Big Data Analytics (BDA) lead to competitive performance gains is given by Mikalef, Pappas, Krogstie, and Giannakos (2018). However, it is argued that the use of big data on a large scale may have unpredictable and undesirable consequences (Corbett 2018).

Biotec is concerned with obtaining products from the extraction or manipulation of living organisms. It is an important industry sector in the economy and in some countries may rank it as the most important sector. The subject does not attract many research studies from accounting/finance academics, but Chander and Mehra (2010) conducted an interesting study of the voluntary disclosure practices of intangible assets of 50 companies in Indian drugs and pharmaceutical industry.

Bitcoins were introduced by a 2008 white paper, "Bitcoin: A Peer-to-Peer Electronic Cash System" (Nakamoto 2014). Bitcoins are a virtual or digital currency. Each Bitcoin is a computer file stored in a "digital wallet" app. on a smartphone or computer. Bitcoins can be sent to your digital wallet and you can make payments. Bitcoins can be used to buy products and services although the number of shops accepting them is small, and some countries have completely banned the use of Bitcoins. The use of Bitcoins has attracted wide attention, and a comprehensive search of the literature by Holub and Johnson (2018) identified 1,206 papers on Bitcoin and these were categorized and mapped across six academic disciplines. Undoubtedly, the use of Bitcoins raises numerous ethical and regulatory considerations (Pasztor 2018). One issue is the high volatility in Bitcoin prices as frequently they are being purchased as a speculative investment. This has raised concerns on its usage as a fiat currency and as a stable and reliable medium of exchange (Thukral 2017).

Black-Scholes Model is an option pricing model that assesses whether option contracts are fairly valued. It states that the value of an option is a function of the short-term interest rate, of the time to exploration, and to the variance of the rate of return on the shares. It is not a function of the expected return on the share. There have been several studies focused on the model. Research by Harikumar and De Boyrie (2004) suggested that the Black-Scholes model outperforms the GARCH models. Choi, Jordan, and Ok (2012) stated that the most widely used option-valuation models among practitioners is the ad hoc Black-Scholes (AHBS) model and their thorough research provides an improvement in the out-of-sample forecast accuracy of the ad hoc Black-Scholes model.

Blockchain is a digital record of transactions made with cryptocurrencies. The name comes from its structure, in which individual records, called blocks, are linked together in single list, called a chain. Blockchains are used for recording transactions made with cryptocurrencies, such as Bitcoin, and it is argued that cryptocurrency is just the first of many opportunities to bring commercial transactions firmly into the 21st century (Weber 2018). It also presents a significant opportunity for economic development (Roberts and Karras 2019). Blockchain is not limited to cryptocurrency and Yang and Hwang (2020) analyses of patents awarded in the United States. Three-quarters of the U.S. blockchain patents were originated in the United States. Half of the awarded U.S. patents are from foreign origin, and the proportion of the blockchain patent originated in the United States is more extensive, suggesting that the United States is a leader in the blockchain technology. The authors also found that 14 percent of blockchain patents were awarded to IBM suggesting that the company is a leader in the blockchain technology.

Blue Chip Stock is the term used for ordinary shares in the most highly regarded companies trading on the stock exchange. The name comes from the highest value chip used in poker. There are innumerable articles on Blue Chip Stocks, but the following explanation by Whitfield (2019) provides a guide to understanding bluechip stocks by identifying the following aspects. They are often among the biggest stocks in sales and/or market cap (share price times the number of shares outstanding). They are thus highly liquid, which means enough shares are available so that placing an order is not a problem. A small investor can slip in and out of a blue chip without making a ripple in the price. They usually pay dividends. Income investors are often attracted to blue chips for the steady payout. Finally, blue chips are usually well-known major companies.

Bollinger Band plots the highest high price and lowest low price of a security over a given time period. It is the centerline with two price channels (bands) above and below it, and the information allow a decision on whether prices of a security can be considered high or low on a relative basis. Bands expand and contract as the price action of an issue becomes volatile (expansion) or becomes bound into a tight trading pattern (contraction). The technique is used in making investment decisions where the assumption is made that the closer the prices move to the upper band, the more overbought the market, and the closer the prices move to the lower band, the more oversold. Gold (2018) found that the portfolio returns improved significantly by including the Bollinger bandwidth (squeeze effect) in the algorithmic trading model.

Bond is a debt obligation (often in the form of a negotiable "note") by a borrower, frequently a government. The bond issuer will pay interest to the holder of the bond at a set rate. Bonds issued by companies are considered riskier than bonds issued by a government and pay a higher rate of interest. Bonds are frequently traded in the stock market and the price can vary. This can be advantageous as, if the market price of the bond reduces, the effective interest rate becomes higher. For example, a $100 bond may pay a return of $6 which gives a return of 6 percent. If the trading value on the market of the bonds declines to $90, the purchaser of the bond at that price will still receive $6, in other words, an interest rate of 6.66 percent. This may be a welcome increase to the holder of the bond but the reason for the decrease in the share price would need to be investigated as it may suggest the company's inability to pay its debts. There are numerous recent articles on bonds, and useful perspectives are given by Spiotto (2019) and Ho and Li (2014).

Book Value is the net value, in an accounting sense, of a company calculated on the total value of its assets less all of its liabilities. The value of an asset is based on the assets in its balance sheet. This is the original cost of the asset less any depreciation, amortization, or impairment costs made against the asset. The relevance and calculation of book values can be complex although an approach to model price as a function of earnings and book values per share addresses that issue. In a study of large Australian and U.S. firms, Clout, Willett, and Smith (2016) found evidence of a higher level of cointegration between market and book values for Australian firms.

Break-Even analysis entails the calculation and examination of the margin of safety for an entity based on the revenues and associated costs. In other words, the analysis shows how many sales it takes to pay for the cost of doing business. Analyzing different price levels relating to various levels of demand, the break-even analysis determines what level of sales are necessary to cover the company's total fixed costs. A demand-side analysis would give a seller significant insight into selling capabilities. Possibly because of its apparent simplicity, the technique attracts little research attention. However, a useful study by Paek (2000) suggests that the technique is a useful method to analyze a company and its branches and applies it to a construction company with branches. The useful application of the technique is wide, and Lemons (2012) suggests that it can help individuals deciding when to file for Social Security as break-even calculations may be tailored to individual and family circumstances and allow for such economic variables such as inflation, return on investment, and current tax rates.

Budgetary Control is used by most organizations no matter how basic the organization. A budget is a quantitative or a financial statement prepared before the start of a trading or financial period. This could be a month or a year. The budgets are for a specific time period and set out the business goals to be met during that period. The budget may be for the entire organization, but it is normal to also set budgets for different departments or activities. The technique has been used for many years, and a study by Berland and Boyns (2002) examines the similarities and differences in France and Britain between the 1920s and the 1960s, outlining the similarities and differences in the experiences of the two countries and examining some of those factors that influenced them. Unfortunately, with budgetary control there comes budgetary slack. The subject of budgetary slack has attracted several research studies, and the influences on creating slack include social pressures, ethical climate, senior management influence, level of participation, and moral justice as identified in the following entry.

Budgetary Slack is the process of padding or setting a budget by overestimating costs and underestimating revenues. A budget designed on this basis gives those who are responsible for working within the budget some slack in the performance levels that should be achieved. It is a subject that has attracted considerable research interest. A study by Özera and Yılmaz (2011) investigated the effects of budgetary control effectiveness, ethical work climate, and managers' procedural justice perception on propensity to create budgetary slack in public organizations. Apriwandi, Yulivia, and Pratiwi (2019) conducted a research experiment to determine the role of management accountants in the creation of budgetary slack. Chong and Sudarso (2016) conducted a laboratory experiment that found under a weak organizational ethical climate, subordinates were more likely to engage in opportunistic behavior and also that budgetary slack creation was lowest in the absence of a peer monitoring control system and where there was a strong organizational ethical climate.

Bull Market is the term used to refer to a strong, healthy stock market. It usually occurs when the demand for a security is greater than the available supply thus causing prices to rise. Bull markets are associated with such factors as a strong or strengthening economy, when the economy is improving. When the market is already strong, there is a sound gross domestic product (GDP) increase in investor confidence, a decrease in unemployment, and an increase in corporate profits. The overall demand for stocks will be positive, and investors will experience confidence. The opposite of a Bull Market is a Bear Market. There is a substantial number of articles on Bear and Bull markets. One that also incorporates Bitcoins is by Bouri, Das, Gupta, and Roubaud (2018).

Business Entity Concept considers that the business is separate from the owner(s) with the business and its owners being treated as two separately identifiable parties. Financial statements are prepared to reflect the activities of the business and not the owners. Although the concept is simple, there are intercountry differences, and some examples are where "special" business entities exist. Most of the literature focuses on business entities in specific countries. There have been several attempts in the United States to define clearly the meaning of "business entity." One committee (Concepts and Standards Research Study Committee) in 1964 concluded that, in discussing underlying concepts, the term "business entity" was unnecessarily restrictive, if not misleading. The underlying concept is identical whether the area of economic interest being accounted for is a "business," a nonprofit organization, governmental unit, or any other form of economic activity. The committee recommended, therefore, that the underlying concept be referred to as the entity concept. This can apply in accounting for "business entities" but is also relevant in accounting for colleges and universities, municipalities, nonprofit hospitals, charitable foundations, and all other classes of "economic entities."

C

Call Option is the right to buy an asset or a financial instrument. Usually, these will be purchased when it is thought that the price of an asset will rise. The sell buyer will only exercise the option if the market price of the asset moves above the exercise price, as the financial benefit is the excess of the market price over the exercise price. If the share price falls below the exercise price, the option will not be exercised. This somewhat brief guide to call options does not reveal the potential complexity of the decision. Ernst (2017) conducted a research that revealed the arbitrage price of a European call option can depend on parameters other than volatility (the standard deviation of the log asset price) and offers two theorems to illustrate this phenomenon. Szu, Wang, and Yang (2015) in a Taiwanese study concluded that the sentiment effect is significantly related to differences between call and put option prices. They suggested that the differential impact of investor sentiment and consumer sentiment on call and put option are due to traders' expectations about underlying asset prices and that rational and irrational sentiment components have different influences on call and put option traders' beliefs.

Callable Bonds are fixed rate bonds, usually convertibles, in which the issuer has the right, but not the obligation, to redeem the bond at par during its life. The call exercise price may be at par, although it is usually set at a premium. A grace period in which the borrower is unable to will usually be in the terms of agreement. A study (Banko and Zhou 2010) covering the period 1980 to 2003 examined the determinants of callable bonds in light of the significant changes in the callable bond market and identified the important causes.

Capacity Utilization is a formula that indicates the extent to which resources are being used at their maximum capacity. The calculation is conducted by expressing the actual output for a period as a percentage of the theoretical maximum output. It is an important ratio as it reveals the impact of fixed overheads per unit on profit margins. High-capacity utilization keeps fixed costs per unit low but low utilization may mean that the total costs per unit are lower than the selling price. This technique is used in many industries. Baumers, Beltrametti, Gasparre, and Hague (2017) examined the manufacturing industry whereas Xiangyong, Rafaliya, Baki, and Chaouch (2017) in a study concerned with medical issues conducted research into the issues of bed capacity and elective surgery.

Capital Asset Pricing Model (CAPM) describes the relationship between systematic risk and expected return for assets, particularly stocks. It is intended to assist companies in choosing its investments and establishing a financing policy to maximize the price or value of its existing equity. CAPM is widely used in finance for pricing risky securities and generating expected returns for assets given the risk of those assets and cost of capital. It is part of portfolio theory but the model has its critics. A very thoughtful article by O'Sullivan (2018) argues that many of the specific criticisms taken individually may be persuasive, but when taken with the efficient market hypothesis (EMH), they contain some highly challengeable if not incoherent presumptions regarding human rationality.

Capital Maintenance Concepts can be financial or physical concepts and determine that a company only generates a profit once the costs associated with operations during a selected accounting period have been fully recuperated. To calculate the profit, the total value of the company's financial and other capital assets at the beginning of the period must be known. The financial concept holds that the capital of a company is only maintained if the financial or monetary amount of its net assets at the end of a financial period is equal to or exceeds the amounts at the beginning of the period excluding any withdrawals or contributions by the owners. To maintain the financial capital, a company has to decide whether adjustments should be made for the purchasing power of money. As for physical capital, it has to be determined whether the funds or resources are equal to or exceeds those at the beginning of the financial period and this excludes any contributions by the owners and any distributions by the company. An interesting article on the development of the concept in the UK is given by Ardern and Aiken (2005).

Capital Reduction occurs where an entity's shareholder equity is reduced either through share cancellations or share repurchases that are also referred to as buybacks. The decision made by a company to reduce its equity can be attributed to such reasons as declining operating profit, increasing shareholder value, and producing a more efficient capital structure. Most of the published literature on the subject focuses on specific examples in various countries. Ryan, Ives, and Dunham (2019) assessed the impacts of price cap regulation—weighted average cost of capital (WACC) reductions on the internal actions of regulated water companies in England and Wales. In a Taiwanese study, Chen, Ho, and Wang (2016) conducted research into earnings management associated with different forms of Capital Reduction.

Cash Equivalents are normally considered as liquid investments having a maturity of three months or less. They are short term, highly liquid investments that are readily convertible into known amounts of cash and should be available for immediate use with a minimal risk of change in value. Examples of cash equivalents include commercial paper, Treasury bills, and short-term government bonds with a maturity date of three months or less. Marketable securities and money market holdings are considered as cash equivalents because they are liquid and not subject to material fluctuations in value. The financial press carries many short articles concerned with cash equivalents that usually address the activities of a particular company. The Journal of Financial Planning reports on research conducted by the Journal of Financial Planning and the FPA Research and Practice Institute TM and sponsored by Longboard Asset Management. The findings of the trend over 10 years revealed that 85 percent of advisers surveyed currently use or recommend to client's cash and cash equivalents and 80 percent currently use or recommend mutual funds.

Cash flow Per Share reveals the ability of a company to pay a dividend to its shareholders. It is calculated by dividing the cash flow by the number of shares in issues. If a cash flow statement required for the decisions is not available, the cash flow per share can be calculated from the Income Statement by assuming that the earnings before interest, tax, depreciation, and amortization (EBITDA) is the equivalent of the "Cash flow." The analysis can be compared to other companies or calculated for several years. If the cash flow per share is a modest amount, investor with ordinary shares may receive only a small dividend, and preference shareholders will receive fixed percentage dividend before ordinary shareholders see any benefits. A study by Kaizoji and Miyano (2019) used a panel regression model for three financial indicators: the dividends per share, cash flow per share, and book value per share, as explanatory variables for share price. They concluded that share prices on average were overvalued in the period from 2005 to 2007 and were undervalued significantly in 2008, when the global financial crisis occurred.

Cash Recovery Rate is used in several situations where the amount of cash being received for an activity is required. The calculation is usually made if there is uncertainty on a company's financial strength. For example, making an investment in machinery and buildings should result in generating more cash than the original costs. There are several methods of making the calculation and one takes the cash flow amount from the cash flow statement and calculates it as a percentage of the current assets or total assets on the balance sheet. The weakness of the approach is that the assets on the balance sheet are shown at their original cost and this may not be any guide to their current worth. The ratio can be used in many situations, for example, assessing payment by customers and the amounts outstanding. Cash flow issues do not attract much academic attention but a well-referenced article by Güleç and Arda (2019) covers 206 nonfinancial firms from four different sectors in Borsa Istanbul (BIST) between the dates of 2008 to 2017. As part of the research, they examined the traditional ratios in different cash flow profiles and the results revealed that liquidity, profitability financial structure, and dividend payout decisions are the functions of cash flow profiles.

Cash Statement shows the actual cash movements in and out for a period of time. It does not show the amount of profit the company has made. The usual format of a Cash Statement would be: Cash Inflows that would usually be the cash and the company has received from the sales it has made and Cash Payments or Outflows that have been made for such items as wages, materials, rent, power, and similar cash outlays so that the business can operate. Although the term "cash" is used, the statement also recognizes other forms of receipts and payments such as checks and bank drafts. Companies complying with international standards are required by IAS 7 *Statement of Cash Flows* to issue a statement of cash flows as an integral part of its primary financial statements. Those complying with U.S. standards are required by Statement of Cash Flows No. 95 (Issued 11/87) to produce a statement showing cash receipts and payments according to whether they stem from operating, investing, or financing activities and provide definitions of each category. There are many articles on cash flow statements. Schmutte and Duncan (2019) provided a useful article on the issues and a study on recent changes in the United States. Stunda (2017) examines differences in reporting cash flow under the International Financial Reporting Standards (IFRS) and the U.S. GAAP statement of cash flow presentation and recognition along with subsequent stock price effect. This study shows that a higher degree of correlation between cash flow and security returns exists for IFRS-based European firms than for GAAP-based U.S. firms, and with respect to security prices, IFRS-based firms appear to be more cash flow sensitive while GAAP-based firms appear to be more accounting earnings sensitive.

Cash to Current Liabilities Ratio divides the total of cash, marketable securities, and cash flow from operating activities by current liabilities. The ratio shows the company's ability to meet short-term financial obligations. An article by Lifland (2010) contends that firms have been emphasizing the days of the working capital cycle. A pool of "'found funds'" exist as the company efficiently manages its current assets and liabilities. A study by Haron and Nomran (2016) highlights the importance of efficient working capital management of a firm regardless of whether it is in time of distress or on daily routine basis.

Chapter 11 of the United States Bankruptcy Code allows reorganization by any business, whether it is a corporation, partnership or sole proprietorship, or even individuals. There have been two recent studies examining Chapter 11 bankruptcy. A recent article by Fisher, Gavious, and Martel (2019) considers the impact of earnings management prior to bankruptcy filing on the movement of firms through Chapter 11, and Jaggia and Thosar (2019) make a useful input to the cost–benefit considerations associated with a Chapter 11 filing.

Chartered Institute of Management Accountants (CIMA) is a UK-based professional body of accountants. The organization provides training and qualification in management accountancy and related subjects and provides ongoing support and training for members. Members of CIMA are usually accountants working in industry.

Chartist is an investor who records past movements of the share price, P/E ratio, turnover, and other financial statistics of individual organizations and constructs charts to predict future share movements. The approach is based on the belief that history repeats itself and that movements of share prices conform to a small number of repetitive patterns. A study by Bazdan (2010) argued that money cannot be managed in the long-term capital stock based solely on technical analysis. He recommended that investors must take into account at least five areas of indicators of fundamental analysis but suggested that the best strategy is "Sell when the violins are playing, buy when the canons rumble."

Common Size Financial Statements demonstrate a method, known as cluster analysis, for analyzing and comparing the financial statements from different companies. The individual elements on the financial statements are expressed as a percentage of the total statements. For example, all the expenditures on a profit statement would be calculated as percentages of the sales figure. The technique was used by Stowe and Stowe (2018) to group credit unions using common size financial statement. This allows the assignment of credit unions to groups by knowing their essential elements but without predefining the groups. Most accounting research focuses on profit statements, but an interesting article by Arnold, Ellis, and Krishnan (2018) develops a common-size analysis framework as the starting point for the financial analysis using the statement of cash flows.

Compliance Audit examines internal control procedures to evaluate how well they operate in practice. In the United States, there are many state-owned or controlled agencies that are required by statutory law to have a biennial audit conducted and released by the Office of the Auditor General (OAG). The extent and depth of audit testing will depend upon the degree to which certain controls are relied upon. There have been various research studies, and one conducted by Nation, Williams, and Buxton (2019) found evidence that supported previous research, and agency size and complexity, measured by audit hours, and the number of prior year findings are statistically significant to the number of compliance audit findings.

Concepts of Capital can be either financial or physical capability, and it is accepted that a profit for a financial period cannot be recognized unless a business has at least maintained the amount of its net assets. The financial capability can be a mixture of a company's long-term debt, short-term debt, common stock, and preferred stock. The physical or operating capacity concept identifies capital as the productive capacity of an entity. A thorough analysis of the history of the concept of capital maintenance in the UK is given by Ardern and Aiken (2005).

Conceptual Framework sets out theoretical principles that form the basis for the regulations of financial accounting and reporting. For many years, those involved with standard setting, whether nationally or internationally, complained that their task was made more difficult by the absence of a unifying structure. A specific accounting problem could arise, and an accounting standard would be issued to address it, but unfortunately, this could create conflict with other regulatory guidance, with no coherence and linking of the individual standards. It was agreed that a framework should be developed based on agreed sets of concepts and principles to guide accounting standard setters. The United States was the first to develop a framework for financial reporting. It is argued that the U.S. framework was mainly concerned with the functioning of the capital markets (Barker and Teixeira 2014). At the international level, the International Accounting Standards Board had to consider practices in many countries that had different histories, industries, and ways of working. The International Accounting Standards Committee (IASC) issued its framework in April 1989, and this was adopted by the International Accounting Standards Board (IASB) in 2001. A revised Conceptual Framework was issued in March 2018 by the IASB and was effective immediately. For companies that use the Conceptual Framework to develop accounting policies, when no IFRS Standard applies to a particular transaction, the revised Conceptual Framework is effective for annual reporting periods beginning on or after January 1, 2020, with earlier application permitted. There have been attempts by the United States and the IASB to agree on one converged conceptual framework but accord has not been reached. Both frameworks are amended from time to time, and the present preachments by FASB are on the following website: www. fasb.org/jsp/FASB/Page/PreCodSectionPage&cid=1176156317989.

A useful article by Walton (2018) comments on papers comparing the two approaches, and an interesting approach by Baker (2017) discusses the influence of accounting theory on FASB's standard setting.

Constructive Obligation is where there is a valid expectation of certain practices on the part of a third party. An example would be where a customer wishes to return purchases and knows that the retail store has had a long-standing policy of allowing customers to return merchandise within, say, a 30-day period. This is a complex area where definitions and explanations rely on those that are used for other terms. Heller (2004) suggests that at the government level, there has been a shift from relatively hard obligations, such as pensions, to obligations and fiscal risk exposures that are more qualitatively and quantitatively uncertain such as medical care and other public services. There is one further category of potential obligations, namely what might be called a government's "implicit contingent liabilities." However, any type of organization can have obligations and a useful guide to the complexity of definitional issues is given in the article by Stuart (2020). The issue has been addressed at the international level by IAS 37 *Provisions, Contingent Liabilities and Contingent Assets* with amendments made to the standard in 2020 that will be effective for annual periods beginning on or after January 1, 2022.

Contingency Theory holds that accounting systems are contingent upon circumstances that prevail at any one time and there are changes in the environment, competition, organizational structures, and technology. It is particularly applied to management accounting systems as it is argued that no single management accounting system is appropriate where there are different conditions in a single organization. A management accounting system is contingent upon the conditions that prevail at any one time in a particular organization. There are several articles on contingency theory and management accounting but a broader and interesting approach is taken by Schweikart (1992) who aligned the theory to the study of ethics in accounting.

Contingent Assets and Liabilities A contingent asset is a possible asset where the existence will be confirmed by the occurrence or nonoccurrence of certain events in the future, which are not wholly in the control of the organization. A contingent liability is a liability where payment is made only if a particular event or circumstance occurs. The IASB in IAS 37 *Provisions, Contingent Liabilities and Contingent Assets* outlines the accounting for provisions (liabilities of uncertain timing or amount), together with contingent assets (possible assets) and contingent liabilities (possible obligations) and presents obligations that are not probable or not reliably measurable. FASB defines a contingency as "An existing condition, situation or set of circumstances involving uncertainty as to possible gain (gain contingency) or loss (loss contingency) to an entity that will ultimately be resolved when one or more future events occur or fail to occur." An interesting article by Franz (2018) examines the case where a company restated its financial statements for the year 2015 due to a disagreement with the Securities and Exchange Commission (SEC) regarding how the firm accounted for unasserted claims related to asbestos litigation that took place almost 60 years earlier.

Convertible Bonds are those issued by an organization, which at the holder's decision, can be converted into shares during the life of the convertible. The exchange ratio (conversion premium) of shares to bonds and the dates on which the conversion can be exercised are fixed in advance. A useful survey of the theoretical and empirical aspects of convertible bond pricing is given by Batten, Khaw, and Young (2014).

Convertible Preferred Shares (stock) give the right to holders to convert the preferred shares into regular common shares under prenegotiated terms and conditions. These shares are corporate fixed-income securities that the investor can choose to turn the preferred shares into a certain number of shares of the company's common stock after a predetermined time span or on a specific date. The fixed-income component offers a steady income stream and some protection of the invested capital. However, the option to convert these securities into stock gives the investor the opportunity to gain from a rise in the share price. Omar and Tang (2019) provided a comprehensive review of the literature and examined earnings management relating to calls of convertible preferred stock.

Core Competencies are the skills and technologies that have been developed throughout an organization. It is the aggregate of the processes by individuals and groups across the learning organization. Prahalad and Hamel (1990) contended that, where companies have areas of significant competitive advantage, these can be used as the structure of the organization's overall strategy. If it is difficult for competitors to replicate these core competencies, they can be exploited to increase customer-perceived value.

Corporate Failure Prediction attempts to apply techniques to assess whether a company is likely to go into liquidation. Altman (1968) devised a multivariate analysis to arrive at a Z-score where a score of 1.8 or less indicated that a company might fail. There are several research articles that have investigated the value of the Z-score for different countries and industries. Although there have been some criticisms of the approach, a recent article (Poudel, Prasad, and Jain 2020) suggests that a Z-score remains applicable to investors and creditors as well as to board members and managers, in identifying if a firm with a higher risk is likely to experience a resultant sharper and stronger negative stock returns.

Corporate Governance is the system by which companies are directed and controlled. A series of financial scandals in North America and Europe in the late 1980s and early 1990s led to national guidelines on corporate governance. Essentially, the guidelines set out the requirements for the rights and responsibilities among different participants in the organization, whose interests the Board of Directors and senior management serve. Boards of Directors are appointed by the shareholders. There are numerous articles, books, and opinions on corporate governance. An article by Gillan (2006) develops a corporate governance framework. A useful and more recent discussion of the research into corporate governance is given by Kumar and Zattoni (2019), and the main concepts of corporate governance, its definitions, objectives, and justifications are provided by Saltaji (2018).

Corporate Social Reporting has become of increasing importance over recent years. At this stage of developments, it can be described as voluntary reporting by organizations to various groups and the public at large on issues that may be considered of general interest and importance. However, various bodies and organizations are issuing advice and suggestions and increasingly environmental, social, and governance (ESG) factors are now of significant interest. (See entry on ESG factors.)

Cost Accounting usually is applied to the methods and techniques for identifying the costs of specific parts of activity in an organization whereas management accounting usually refers on the provision of financial information to managers. Although the terms management accounting and cost accounting are sometimes used interchangeably, originally the term cost accounting was the one used. In 1919, accountants in the United States held a meeting and the National Association of Cost Accountants was formed. This was later to become the Institute of Management Accountants (Parks 2019). The different methods of cost accounting are explained by Hussey and Ong (2018).

Cost Benefit Analysis is a technique that takes into account the estimated costs to be incurred by a proposed investment or activity and the estimated benefits. The benefits may be due to an increase in revenue from a product or service or from a reduction in costs. The analysis may also include by such factors as the impact on the environment or a reduction in accidents. An article by Bradshaw (2019) compares and contrasts cost-benefit analysis with "collaborative analysis." It explains the fundamentals of collaborative analysis and the benefits it offers to agencies, stakeholders, and courts.

Cost of Capital can be defined as the weighted cost of equity reflecting the return that the investor is looking for when deciding to buy shares. However, there are various ways of defining the phrase and a company's capital structure can be defined as equity plus various sources of debt. Baule (2019) argues that the cost of debt is an essential component of the cost of capital, which is a central figure in a number of applications, such as capital budgeting, performance measurement, and firm valuation. Another view would be to calculate the weighted average cost of capital (WACC) where the calculation is weighted by market values (International Accountant 2017). This approach has been extended by Olson and Pagano (2017) who have proposed a new way to measure the cost of capital, called the Empirical Average Cost of Capital (EACC). The authors claim that this is consistent with the existing methods of calculating the WACC, but uses information from the firm's financial statements and requires fewer and less subjective inputs.

Cost-Plus Pricing is method of pricing products or services where on the total costs (variable and fixed) is added a percentage amount to derive the market price. This is known as the cost-plus model. This method can only be used if the market is noncompetitive or only slightly competitive, but it ensures that a company can recover all its costs and make a profit. However, there are competitors and consumers with their own objectives. The competitors may be able to charge less for their products and the consumers will usually have a set price above which they will not go. There are other factors that need to be considered. Changes may have occurred in the market environment where the company has operated or intends to do so and there may be competition from others who have adopted the strategy of cost leadership. There is also the real possibility that customers may place a different value on the product or service than the company has and will attempt to drive down the market price. Despite these potential drawbacks, cost plus pricing remains a popular technique. The logic for its use is simple. To continue to exist, an organization must make a profit. Failure to do so will result in bankruptcy. Given the number of years that the technique has been used, not surprisingly there are many articles on its use. A very well-referenced article that examines the use of the technique in World War 1 is by Volmers, Antonelli, D'Alessio, and Rossi (2016). A more recent view that applies a theory of pricing in consumer markets that relates cost-plus pricing and value-based pricing to price competition and price leadership, including, in particular, competitive price leadership is given by Farm (2020).

Cost–Volume–Profit (CVP) Analysis is a decision-making technique for analyzing the interrelationship among sales price, volume, and the impact on profitability due to changes in fixed or variable costs. It is applied to determine the level of activity required to determine whether a proposed activity will be profitable. Said (2016) suggests that as CVP analysis is based on statistical models, decisions can be broken down into probabilities that help with short-term decision-making objectives and explores, investigates, and applies the CVP model to four different statistical distributions.

Creditor Payment Period is an efficiency ratio that measures the average time that the business has taken to pay its trade creditors. The creditor payment period in days is calculated using the following formula:

$$\frac{\text{Trade creditors}}{\text{Purchases}} \times 365.$$

Although some people do not like debts and prefer to pay invoices and statements soon as they receive them rather than wait until they are due, this is not always a prudent method for managing cash. Receiving goods on credit is the equivalent of having an interest-free loan. If the supplier does not give credit, the business may have to go into overdraft to pay cash for the goods. This does not mean that a business should wait until it receives a solicitor's letter or risk supplies being cut off, but from a financial point of view, management should take the maximum time allowed to pay trade creditors while at the same time collect payment from trade debtors as quickly as possible. The premise underpinning these ratios is that companies should be able to pay their current liabilities from their current assets. If they are unable to do so, they must seek more finance. The situation can be difficult if the economy is in decline or its future strength uncertain. However, not all countries may have the same approach and the published articles tend to focus on one country or industry and with the focus on working capital. For example, a study of countries found that Canadian firms invest less in working capital than their U.S. counterparts (Khokhar 2019).

Crypto Currencies are not metal or paper currencies with a physical presence. Crypto currencies are virtual and digital money that take the form of tokens or "coins" and exist only on a distributed and decentralized ledger. Users make secure payments and store money without the need to use their name or go through a bank. Individual coin ownership records are stored in a computerized database to secure transaction records, to control the creation of additional coins, and to verify the transfer of coin ownership. The use of crypto currencies has expanded significantly since Bitcoin was launched. A good guide to understanding the Bitcoin currency is by Smith and Kumar (2018) and includes the issues regarding taxation in the United States. Skarlatos and Plum (2018) have raised the question whether reporting the currency in the United States is sufficiently stringent and one can anticipate that this is an area for further discussion. Some examples of crypto currencies include Bitcoin Cash, Ethereum, Ripple, Litecoin, Cardano, Dogecoin.

Current Cost Accounting is a method in which the concept of capital maintenance is based on securing the operating capability of a business.

Assets are valued at their deprival value this being their worth to the business. The value of an asset can be calculated on the loss the organization would suffer, which may be the cost of replacing it, the value if it were sold, or its economic value to the business. Although the technique may be used in particular decision-making situations, it has not been established as an alternative to historical cost accounting. Taylor, Nunley, and Flock (2004) suggested that managers in manufacturing may use information based on current cost accounting methods to make business decisions. Their approach was a method to determine inventory valuation that is essential so that managers can understand the implications and market value of Work-In-Process (WIP) and how it affects their business.

Current Ratio shows the relationship between the business's liquid (current) assets and its current liabilities. In other words, it shows whether the company looks able to pay its current debts without seeking loans. Inventory (stock) is a current asset but it has to be sold before you can turn it into cash. It is therefore normal practice to use current assets minus the value of stock when calculating the current test. Similarly, only the creditors who have to be paid within the next 12 months are considered as this is our present concern. If there are creditors that have to be paid after 12 months, this is a separate and less urgent consideration. One calculation, although there are variations of this, is

$$\frac{\text{Current assets - Inventory}}{\text{Creditors with amounts due within one yeae}}.$$

This ratio is widely used in practice and is also incorporated into many research studies in different countries and industries. Examples are an emerging Asian economy (Rahman and Hossain 2020), the oil industry in Indonesia (Herdyanto and Yudawisastra 2019), cement companies in India (Muthusamy and Karthika 2019), and external financial balances in the European Union (Afonso, Huart, Jalles, and Stanek 2019).

D

Dashboards in the workplace are similar to a car dashboard that informs the driver about, speed, fuel consumption, temperature, and similar information. Dashboards are increasingly being used in several situations to provide a quick information source in the workplace. Dashboards serve a similar purpose as other management tools that visually track, analyze, and display performance indicators (KPI), metrics and data that show the current operation of a business, department, or specific process. They are used in many industries and organizations such as higher education (McCoy and Rosenbaum 2019) and supply chain management in the oil and gas industries (Magnus and Rudra 2019). Some would regard the use of dashboards as a contribution to management decision making. A helpful review of four books discussing advances in management techniques is given by Gray (2006).

Data Analytics is the science of examining raw data for information and decision-making purposes. An algorithmic or mechanical process is used. Data analytics is now applied in several industries to allow organizations and companies to make better decisions as well as verify and disprove existing theories or models. The focus of data analytics lies in inference, which is the process of deriving conclusions from a substantial amount of data that is already available. An article by Batistic and van der Laken (2019) examines the development of Data Analytics and its future potential in investigating organizational performance, and Raguseo and Vitari (2018) explained the forms of business value that companies can create from Data Analytics investments.

Debenture are long-term debt instruments that are corporate securities and repayable at a fixed date. A debenture is normally backed by the general credit of the issuer rather than by a lien on specific assets. The order of any prior claims is set forth in the debenture. Typically, in the event of liquidation, debentures have a low recovery ranking. A useful article on debt instruments and cash flows by Wampler and Smolinski

(2018) discusses the Accounting Standards Update (ASU) No. 2016-15, Classification of Certain Cash receipts, and Cash payments issued by the Financial Accounting Standards Board FASB. An unusual and comprehensive example of the issue of bonus debentures is given by Chaklader and Aggarwal (2011). Bonus shares are issued to the shareholders by capitalizing the reserves and thus nothing is charged from the shareholders. These debentures are free of cost.

Debt Collection Period is an efficiency ratio that gives an indication of the effectiveness of the management of working capital. It measures the average time trade debtors (customers) have taken to pay the business for goods and services bought on credit over the year. The debtor collection period in days is calculated using the following formula:

$$\frac{\text{Trade debtors}}{\text{Turnover}} \times 365.$$

If a breakdown of debtors is not given in the balance sheet, it is likely that the figure for trade debtors is given in the notes to the accounts. Possibly, because academics consider the subject mundane, there are very few published studies but Korkmaz (2017) provides an interesting study into the relations between the debt structure and the profitability of firms in the context of the Istanbul Stock Exchange.

Debt Equity Ratio, also known as the leverage or gearing ratio, analyses the financial structure of a business. The long-term debt is calculated as a percentage of the amount of equity of a company or as the ratio of the debt to the total of debt plus equity. A high leverage (geared) organization has a debt higher than the amount of its equity in comparison to similar organizations. Although it may offer a higher return to investors when it is performing well, it reports a loss very quickly when there is an economic downturn. A study by Ataullah, Higson, and Tippett (2007) examined the quasi-supply side model of a firm by testing the prediction that the evolution of a firm's debt to equity ratio will be compatible with a nonlinear (target adjustment) process whose underlying probability density function possesses no convergent moments. A somewhat dated article by Kormendi (1983) is of interest as it deals specifically with U.S. government spending and savings.

Decision Trees are used in many disciplines and in businesses and are usually in the form of a model, chart, or diagram showing the elements in a business decision. They are frequently shown diagrammatically as a tree with various branches and help explore all of the decision alternatives and their possible outcomes. The diagrams assist in determining a course of action or may show a statistical probability. There are several articles demonstrating the application of decision trees in making business decisions but the scope is wide and even includes a proposal on how to evaluate defensive actions against terrorist attacks in a dynamic and hostile environment (Garcia and von Winterfeldt 2016). Possibly, a more applicable suggestion is given by Nor, Ismail, and Yap (2019) who developed a personal bankruptcy prediction model using the decision tree technique.

Defensive Interval Ratio is used in several different situations. For example, it might be used to calculate the ability of a business to satisfy its current debts by determining the length of time it can operate on current liquid assets without needing revenue. The calculation is current assets less stock divided by the projected daily operational expenditure less noncash charges. The projected daily operational expenditure is usually calculated by dividing the total of the cost of goods sold, operating expenses, and other cash expenses by 365. An important industry, but usually ignored by researchers, is the trading and repairs of vehicles, and an informative study by Baciu and Brezeanu (2018) provides substantial data on their financial position over several years including liquidity indicators.

Deflation Risk is the opposite of inflation where there is a general increase in prices. A study by Fleckenstein, Longstaff, and Lustig (2017) concluded from their investigations that the opinion that the risk of economic downturn is severe enough to result in deflation is fundamentally related to the risk of major shocks in the financial markets, both locally and globally. The many articles examining deflation in various countries and industries demonstrate that deflation is experienced more widely than many would expect.

Derivatives are financial instruments that can be traded (e.g., options, warrants, rights, futures contracts, options on futures) on various markets. They are called derivatives because they are "derived" from some real, underlying item of value (such as a company share or other real, tangible commodity). A derivative is a tradable "contract," created by exchanges and dealers. A warrant or option is the simplest form of derivative. The most common usage relates to the trading of commodity futures and options on futures where predefined contracts relating to a right to buy or sell and underlying commodity or security are traded as opposed to the actual commodity or security itself. They are risky because they are time-fused and can expire worthless. There are many academic articles on the subject. A recent study by Abugri and Osah (2021) focuses on U.S. banks, and a 30-year perspective on property derivatives is given by Fabozzi, Shiller, and Tunaru (2020).

Digital Wallets permit individuals or businesses to make transactions electronically. There are numerous articles reporting on the adoption of digital wallets in different countries and the use by people of different ages and backgrounds. A most comprehensive review of digital wallets is given by Levitin (2018) who concludes that although they can develop a beneficial reshaping of retail commerce, there must be a fair and competitive marketplace is key to realizing on that promise.

Discounted Cash Flows is a method that forecasts the amount of cash inflows and outflows over the life of a project and discounts them to present value, based on a selected interest rate. The Editorial of the Journal of Applied Accounting Finance observes that "The concept of risk has been an integral part of corporate finance theory since at least 1938, when John Burr Williams' book The Theory of Investment Value was published. This volume introduced the DCF model to value not only bonds but common stocks by discounting future dividends to the present" (McCormack 2018). Several appraisal methods use the DCF approach including the net present value (NPV), the internal rate of return, and the profitability index.

Disinflation is a term used and mostly preferred by governments, possibly because it sounds less painful than deflation. A useful introduction to the literature on the subject is given by Tesfaselassie (2019). A discussion of the policy challenges that a country faces when it, understandably, wants to both reduce inflation and maintain a sustainable external position is provided by Tanner (2019).

Dividend Cover Ratio shows the potential ability of a company to continue to pay dividends in the future. It is calculated by dividing the profits available currently for distribution by the amount of the dividend. A low ratio suggests that a company may not be able to continue to pay the same dividend in the future and a high ratio leads to the opposite conclusion.

Dividend Yield Ratio shows a comparison of dividends received with other forms of investments. It is calculated by expressing the dividends paid per share as a percentage of the market price of ordinary shares. It is normal practice to calculate the gross dividend yield so that a direct comparison can be made with gross interest yields from other forms of investment. An article that focuses on dividends at a particular stage is by Chiek and Akpan (2016). Their research provides statistically significant, quantitative variables that determine the share price of oil and gas sector companies listed on the Nigerian Stock Exchange, during the economic slowdown period of 2009 to 2013.

Dogecoin (DOGE) is a joke cryptocurrency created by software engineers Billy Markus and Jackson Palmer in 2013. (Couts, *December 12, 2013*). Dogecoin features the face of the Shiba Inu dog from the "Doge" meme as its logo and namesake. Unlike Bitcoin, which is designed to be scarce, Dogecoin is intentionally abundant: 10,000 new coins are mined every minute and there is no maximum supply. *Dogecoin.com* promotes the currency as the "fun and friendly internet currency". Despite its satirical nature, some consider it a legitimate investment prospect, reaching a market capitalization in excess of U.S. $85 billion in May, 2021.

Double Entry Book-Keeping is the hurdle that confronts every first-year accounting student. A critical milestone in accounting was the publication in Venice in 1494 of Pacioli's Summa de Arithmetica Geometria Proportioni et Proportionalita (Sangster and Scataglinibelghitar 2010). This identified a system of keeping financial records which revolutionized commerce throughout Europe. We still use the same principles today as an indication that an organization may not be able to develop as reflected by the accounting equation. It is claimed that Pacioli developed a sound, straightforward, and reliable principles-based method of instruction in double entry. The evidence for this statement can be found in an extremely well-referenced article by Sangster (2018).

Dow Jones Industrial Average (DJIA) is the second oldest U.S. market and tracks 30 large, publicly owned blue chip companies trading on the New York Stock Exchange (NYSE) and the NASDAQ. It is named after Charles Dow, who created the index back in 1896 along with his business partner Edward Jones. A study by Jong, Elfayoumy, and Schnusenberg (2017) concluded that traders concerned with the DJIA would be advised to refer to social media and to follow Twitter activity throughout the day to better gauge the behavior of the stock in the immediate future.

Due Diligence generally refers to an action being undertaken with reasonable care and can refer to several different human activities. In relation to accounting, it is an investigation, audit, or review performed to confirm the facts which usually involves an examination of financial records before entering into a proposed transaction with another party. An article by Preusch (2015) discusses the importance of due diligence for accounting firms in the United States to avoid civil penalties and sanctions under the Internal Revenue Service's (IRS) requirement to exercise due diligence when preparing IRS documents. Many of the articles on due diligence are based on the health industry, in all its forms, in the United States. The issue is far broader both in content and location than the health industry as demonstrated by an insightful and unusual article by Ortner (2015) on cybercrime and the Russian mafia.

DuPont Analysis is widely used to examine the different drivers of a company's performance and assists investors in identifying its strengths and weaknesses. The analysis uses the following financial equation:

$$\text{net profit margin} \times \text{asset turnover} \times \text{equity multiplier,}$$

which is a combination of three other ratios. There are several articles on the application of the DuPont model and a U.S.-based research article concludes that there is a practical shortcoming in the application of DuPont ratios and, more broadly, efficiency ratios that use information that is not measured on a consistent monetary basis (Curtis, Lewis-Western, and Toynbee 2015).

E

Earnings Management may be conducted by companies and not always be detected by auditors. It may even be referred to as "income smoothing" and therefore it is not possible to identify the degree and type of earnings management. One view held in the United States is that the distortion of the application of GAAPs, and Meisel (undated) suggests that it has been with us for many years. Because of the importance of calculating the EPS, a complete and workable definition is required. The accounting standard setters are currently examining the issue, and the SEC is focusing on quarter-end transactions or accounting adjustments done primarily or solely by public companies to meet desired financial metrics (Scheck 2020).

Earnings Per Share (EPS) is calculated by dividing the profit or loss attributable to ordinary equity holders of the parent entity (the numerator) by the weighted average number of ordinary shares outstanding (the denominator) during the period. This includes all ordinary shares in issue during the year. The ratio provides information to shareholders on the dividend they may receive. If a company is paying high dividends, the shareholder not only has an immediate return but the share price may also increase as it is a successful company. In the United States, the Financial Accounting Standards Board FASB has issued the Accounting Standards Codification (ASC) 260, Earnings per Share EPS. A post-implementation review team with the Financial Accounting Foundation found that the standard has accomplished its objectives of simplifying computations of EPS and achieving more comparability with international accounting standards (Journal of Accountancy 2016). At the international level, IAS 33 provides guidance for calculating and presenting the information. However, there are criticisms of using EPS as a measure of performance and Almeida (2019) argues that the measure appears to lead to long-term underperformance and can significantly affect economic growth and welfare. A research study by Chapman and Green (2018) concluded that analysts ask managers for forward-looking information in one-third of quarterly conference calls and most frequently are seeking EPS guidance. They conclude that analysts shape managers' disclosure choices in meaningful ways.

Economic Order Quantity (EOC) is a mathematical model that determines the optimal amount of inventory to be ordered while minimizing the total ordering and holding costs. EOQ is computed as follow:

ECQ = (square root of 2AD/H), where the EOQ is the optimal quantity to be purchased, A is the cost for processing an order, D is the quantity required for a particular period, and H is the holding cost per unit of the inventory.

An article by Shekarian, Olugu Abdul-Rashid, and Kazemi (2016) focuses on an EOQ model for items with imperfect quality based on two different holding costs and learning considerations. Moily (2015) identifies the various models used and the economic framework for profit maximization and develops an Economic Manufacturing Quantity (EMQ) for integrating the other approaches.

Economic Value Added (EVA) is a financial performance measure used to evaluate a company's true profit and is a trademark of Stern Stewart & Co. There is a website dedicated to so-called EVAnomics at www. evanomics.com. EVA is often called economic profit (EP) to avoid problems caused by trademarking. EP has been defined as total net gains less the interest on invested capital at the current rate. The reason for this calculation is that shareholders must earn a return that compensates for the risk taken. Equity capital has to earn at least the same return as similarly risky investments in the equity markets. There have been several studies that have considered the use of EVA as a financial performance measure. A recent review of the literature by Obaidat (2019) explains that shareholders value maximization is of considerable importance, but traditional accounting measures have been criticized because they failed to represent fully the factors that drive shareholder value. Obaidat suggests that EVA is used with the traditional accounting measures because they are not considered as substitutes for each other. Instead, EVA should be seen as an enhancement to the traditional accounting measures, which if used properly with them, will provide a more powerful tool to evaluate the performance.

Efficient Market Hypothesis (EMH) assumes that share prices reflect all information and trade at their fair value on stock exchanges. If applying this hypothesis, it is argued that it is impossible for investors to purchase undervalued stocks or sell stocks for inflated prices. In an article on the qualitative and quantitative history of the EMH, Jovanovic (2018) states that the definition and the scope of this hypothesis have been modified several times. This conclusion is also identified by O'Sullivan (2018) who suggest that although the related Capital Asset Pricing Model (CAPM) and Efficient Markets Hypothesis are twin theories that may be able to withstand many of the specific criticisms taken individually, a critical philosophical assessment leads to the conclusion that they are empirically falsified and have some highly challengeable, if not incoherent presumptions, regarding human rationality.

Embedded Derivative is a derivative that is part of a hybrid financial instrument including both the derivative and a host contract. With this type of instrument compared to a stand-alone derivative, some of the cash flows vary. The issue is addressed in International Accounting Standard 39 and in the U.S. ASU No. 2016-06, Derivatives and Hedging (Topic 815): Contingent Put and Call Options in Debt Instruments. U.S. GAAP requires embedded derivatives to be separated from the host contract and accounted for separately as derivatives if certain criteria are met. It clarifies that when a call or put option is contingently exercisable, an entity does not have to assess whether the event that triggers the ability to exercise a call or put option is related to interest rates or credit risks. The amendments came into effect for the financial statements of public business entities that were issued for fiscal years beginning after December 15, 2016, and interim periods within those fiscal years. For other entities, the amendments came into effect for financial statements issued for the fiscal years beginning after December 15, 2017, and interim periods within fiscal years beginning after December 15, 2018. A thoughtful article by Abdel-Khalik (2019) discusses the IFRS and the codified accounting standards (ASC) for U.S. GAAP.

Environmental, Social, and Governance (ESG) factors is a relatively recent approach to corporate reporting that discusses the importance of these factors on business activities. ESG has developed into a significant factor in discussions on corporate reporting in general and attracted numerous articles. A study by Yu, Guo, and Luu (2018) examines the extent of ESG disclosure and the possible impact on firm value. In a more recent study, Capelle-Blancard and Petit (2020) conducted a substantial research project to identify the extent and the determinants of the stock market's reaction following ordinary news related to ESG issues. Interestingly, a Sustainability Accounting Standards Board (SASBs), which is not directly associated with financial accounting standards regulations, has been established and is discussed later in this *Guide*.

Equity in its broadest sense can be defined as a beneficial interest in an asset. In accounting and finance terms, it is the shareholders' stake in a company and the term is used in several key financial ratios. The amount of equity is shown on company's balance sheet and also can be calculated by deducting company's total liabilities from its total assets. Note that the term equity does not refer to the current market price of any shares. The term is often used synonymously with "shareholding" or "stakeholding" and is sometimes used synonymously with "security." It is also used more broadly in various disciplines with terms such as gender equity. Not surprisingly, accounting and finance references to the subject of equity attracts numerous articles. A recent article that provide substantial research and well-argued opinions is by Nagaraj and Zhang (2019).

Escrow is a legal concept that describes a financial instrument where an asset or escrow money is held by a third party on behalf of two other parties that are in the process of completing a transaction. Escrow accounts might include escrow fees where managed by agents who hold the funds or assets until receiving appropriate instructions or until the fulfillment of predetermined contractual obligations. Money, securities, funds, and other assets can all be held in escrow. A similar process would be a fully funded documentary letter of credit. It is often suggested as a replacement for a certified or cashier's check.

Exchange Traded Fund is a security that follows an index, sector, or commodity. They are important investments as they can be purchased or sold on a stock exchange the same as a regular stock. A very useful article by Lettau and Madhavan (2018) claims that ETFs are one of the most important financial innovations in decades and recent issues in the market place, such as Bitcoins, and how they may be resolved are explained by Halsey and Halsey (2020).

Exit Strategy refers to the way in which investors and founders can "exit," that is, leave their company with a cash return on their investment. The examples are going public, being acquired or being bought out by other shareholders. The term is also widely used in various nonfinancial situations. Fuh and Luo (2018) gave advice where there is an exit strategy.

Expanded Accounting Equation is based on the accounting equation but gives more detail of the different components of stockholder equity, also known as capital, in a company. It is the shareholders who own the company and the profit belongs to them. It may be distributed or retained in the company to provide growth. In the expanded accounting equation, the total amount for capital (equity) is broken down into its various segments thus providing analysts with information on the division of profit made by a company. Essentially, profit for a period is used to pay dividends to the shareholders, reinvested in the company, or retained as cash. One simple formula is as follow:

$$\text{Assets - liabilities = Capital originally invested by}$$
$$\text{shareholders profit for the period - dividends paid.}$$

There are variations on this but the intent is to focus on changes in shareholders' equity. The topic is of importance to first year accounting students and sometimes addressed in the educational literature.

eXtensible Business Reporting Language (XBRL) enables companies to release financial and business information in a format that can be quickly, efficiently, and cost effectively accessed, sorted and analyzed over the Internet. It provides a language in which reporting terms can be authoritatively defined. Those reporting terms can then be used to uniquely represent the contents of financial statements or other kinds of compliance, performance, and business reports. XBRL facilitates reporting information to move between organizations rapidly, accurately, and digitally. The FASB has published the 2020 FASB Taxonomy Implementation Guides (Guides) that offer insight on the application of the U.S. GAAP financial reporting taxonomy to financial statements and notes disclosures. The position in the United States, can be found on www.fasb.org/jsp/FASB/Page/SectionPage&cid=1176157087972.

The international view can be found on www.ifrs.org/issued-standards/ ifrs-taxonomy/ifrs-taxonomy-illustrative-examples/.

F

Fair Value is the amount of consideration that can be agreed for an asset or a liability to be exchanged or settled in an arm's length transaction between informed and willing parties. Fair value hedges are derivatives or other financial instruments to hedge potential changes in the fair value of the whole or part of a recognized asset or liability. The position internationally is covered in IAS 39 and in the United States by SFAS 133. In a well-referenced article, Frestad (2018) proposed a model that shows how nonfinancial firms that prefer predictable earnings jointly optimize their hedging strategy and the choice between fair value and hedge accounting.

Fair Value Accounting has been advocated by standard setters who argue that fair values are more relevant and have advocated measuring all financial instruments at fair value (Financial Accounting Standards Board (FASB) 1998, 2006, 2010a). However, under current generally accepted accounting principles (GAAP), the majority of financial instruments should be measured using historical cost. Surprisingly, there is little evidence on whether measuring financial instruments using fair value in lieu of current GAAP enhances overall financial statement relevance. The available literature on the subject has explored whether fair values of financial instruments have incremental value relevance beyond that of historical costs (Landsman 2007). In contrast, less attention has been paid to the relative value relevance, which is critical when policy makers must make "either/or" choices among competing accounting methods (Biddle, Seow, and Siegel 1995). McInnis, Yu, and Yust (2018) compared the value relevance of banks' financial statements (balance sheets and income statements) under fair value and current GAAP.

Fiat Currency is government-issued currency that is not backed by a physical commodity, such as gold or silver, but rather by the government that issued it. The value of fiat money is derived from the relationship between supply and demand and the stability of the issuing government, rather than the worth of a commodity backing it as is the case for commodity money. Most modern paper currencies are fiat currencies, including the U.S. dollar, the euro, and other major global currencies. Kirkby (2018) argued that digital fiat money would be an imprudent move as it makes the central bank responsible for the entire money supply. Hong, Park, and Yu (2018) provided a useful review of the literature and have developed a theoretical model of monetary economics.

Financial Accounting Standards Board (FASB) The FASB was founded in 1973 following the recommendations of the 1972 Wheat Committee of the American Institute of Certified Public Accountants (AICPA). The FASB was a different type of organization from its predecessor, the Accounting Principles Board (APB), which was controlled by the accounting profession. The FASB had the responsibility of acting in the best interests of the main financial statement users, deemed to be investors and is authorized by the SEC. This is an unusual relationship as the FASB is a private-sector organization but under the careful surveillance of the SEC. The accounting standards issued by the FASB are recognized as authoritative and generally accepted for the purposes of U.S. federal securities laws. There has been a significant change in the operation of the FASB. From 1973 to 2009, the FASB issued 168 SFASs. On July 1, 2009, the FASB ASC was launched. ASCs are issued to amend the codification. The FASB ASC is now the official source of authoritative, nongovernmental GAAP. It has three levels. Each *Topic* contains at least one *Subtopic* containing *Sections* that include the actual accounting guidance. Sections are based on the nature of the content (e.g., scope, recognition, and measurement) and are standardized throughout the codification. Each Section includes numbered Paragraphs commencing with the Section number followed by the unique paragraph number. Additions to U.S. GAAP are issued by means of a FASB document called an ASU. These bring changes in the ASC and therefore in U.S. GAAP. A useful guide to the codification system has been published by PricewaterhouseCoopers and this was updated in 2017 (PwC). For the FASB in the United States, the login is www.fasb.org/academics.

Financial Instability Hypothesis is attributed to Minsky (1992) who argued that real (market) analysis and financial (market) analysis should be analyzed together, not separately; and that the macroeconomy is inherently unstable. A very thorough and helpful explanation of the hypothesis is given by Miller (2018). Troncoso (2019) concentrated on the 2008 financial crisis to examine two major competing theoretical explanations of the crisis, and Sofoklis and Constantinos (2019) contended that Bitcoin exhibited the formation of a speculative bubble in 2017.

Financial Instruments are monetary contracts between parties that give rise to a financial asset of one party and a financial liability or equity instrument of another party. Examples are futures, options contracts, and bills of exchange. The accounting for financial instruments is covered by IAS 39 for international applications and SFAS No. 133 for U.S. GAAP. The attempts of the regulators are not always met with approval, and A. Rashad (2019) argued that setting standards for financial reporting has gone astray with standard-setting bodies being overwhelmed and fascinated by the precise financial engineering models, although these may be inappropriate. Another paper focusing on IAS 32 explores various approaches that may be pursued by the standard setters to improve accounting in this area and identify areas for future research (Farghera, Sidhub, Tarcac, and van Zyel 2019).

Financial Technology (Fintech) is used to describe new technology that seeks to improve and automate the delivery and use of financial services. At its core, fintech is applied to assist companies, business owners, and consumers to better manage their financial operations, processes by utilizing specialized software and algorithms that are used on computers and, increasingly, smartphones. The term Fintech was initially applied to the technology employed at the back-end systems of established financial institutions. Since then, there has been a shift to more consumer-oriented services and a more consumer-oriented definition. Fintech now includes different sectors and industries such as education, retail banking, fundraising and nonprofit, and investment management. Fintech also includes the development and use of crypto-currencies such as Bitcoin. While that segment of Fintech may see the most headlines, the big money still lies in the traditional global banking industry and its multitrillion-dollar market capitalization. There are numerous articles on the subject; Chen, Wu, and Yang (2019) provided substantial evidence on the occurrence and value of FinTech innovation, and Luther (2020) argued that a national Fintech charter is the best approach to ensuring that consumers who rely on these loans receive the full protections guaranteed by federal law.

First-in First-out (FIFO) has attracted several articles that are concerned with the use of nonresident workers (NRWs) who are part of the FIFO employment practices (Cameron and Pfeiffer 2014). However, our interest in this *Guide* is concerned with a very different subject. We are discussing FIFO as a method of valuing units of raw material or finished goods issued from inventory. It is based on the earliest unit value for pricing the materials issued to production until all the inventory at that price has been used up. The next latest price is then used until all the inventory at that price is used for pricing the issues. FIFO is also used in process costing to value the Work In Progress (WIP) at the end of the period. The application of the method becomes more difficult with perishable inventory. In this instance, a company orders a product with a positive lead time and sells it to multiple demand classes, each only accepting products with remaining lifetime longer than a threshold. This is a problem studied by Hossein, OpherOded, and Chen (2019) who suggest helpful solutions.

Five Forces Model was developed by Porter (1985) and can be helpful in determining the strategy of an organization. He proposed that the following competitive forces affect a company's profits:

1. The threat of new entrants into an industry or market served by a specific company;
2. The bargaining power of suppliers;
3. The bargaining power of the consumer;
4. The threat of substitute products or services; and
5. The intensity of rivalry among existing companies.

An article by Prasad and Warrier (2016) examines the world of Increasing Returns to Scale, within the realms of Strategic Management and argues that Michael Porter's Five Forces Model is a static model and becomes difficult to apply to an industry stage where all the five forces have a propensity to keep changing. However, an interesting article by Zhang, Leng, and Zhou (2020) demonstrates how they used the model to study social enterprises that create value by focusing on challenging social problems. This is an approach that aims to solve the dual problems of service effectiveness and market demand.

Fixed Assets Turnover Ratio is used to evaluate an organization's level of activity over a specified period. The ratio is calculated by dividing revenues by the balance sheet value of the noncurrent assets that may be taken at the beginning or end of the period or the average of the two. The higher the turnover ratio, the more active and efficient the organization is considered to be. A study by Babaei and Shahveisi (2017) concluded that the fixed asset turnover ratio, amongst others, had no impact on market value. It should not be concluded from this that the ratio has no value and research by Shumaila and Tahir (2020) concluded that there is a high impact of financing costs and low impact of fixed asset turnover ratio on the profitability of the textile industry of Pakistan.

Form 10k is required to be filed annually by publicly traded corporations with the Securities and Exchange Commission (SEC). Comprehensive information is required, including audited financial statements. The information on the Form 10k is more detailed but similar to the annual report and accounts. An interesting article by Mitra, Al-Hayale, and Hossain (2019) examines the issues arising from companies submitting late Form 10k.

Free Cash Flow Ratio focuses on operating cash flows because, as well as paying dividends, there is also the shareholders' expectations that a company may grow and become even more profitable. There is also the issue that a company may not have sufficient cash to survive a difficult economic climate. The answer to these problems is the operating cash flow ratio. Some analysts deduct capital expenditures from this amount as they argue that these are necessary to maintain the company's activities. The amount of free cash flow that has been identified can be compared to previous years either using a trend analysis or comparing to other companies. The ratio can be calculated using the following formula:

$$\frac{\text{Free cash flow}}{\text{Operating cash flow}}.$$

If a company has a high percentage of free cash flow, it is interpreted as being financially stable as it has financial strength. Although the ratio may not be as well used as those that are profit-based, Bowden and Posch (2011) argued that managerial bonuses and shareholder dividends should be treated more symmetrically and constrained by free cash flow criteria that capture producer surplus created by genuine managerial ability.

Future Contracts are bought and sold on organized exchanges. The contracts take the form of an agreement to buy or sell a fixed quantity of a particular commodity, currency, or security for delivery at a fixed date at a fixed price in the future. Unlike an option, a futures contract involves a definite purchase or sell and not only an option. Therefore, may be the disadvantage of a potentially unlimited loss. Future contracts, however, provide an opportunity for those who purchase goods regularly to hedge against increased changes in prices. For hedges to be possible, there must be speculators willing to offer these contracts. Future contracts can reduce financial risk but usually do not result from gains in favorable movements in the prices of underlying instruments. A study by Salvador and Arago (2014) estimates linear and nonlinear GARCH models to find optimal hedge ratios with futures contracts for some of the main European stock indexes.

G

GameStop Corporation is an American video game, consumer electronics, and gaming merchandise retailer and the name to which many will attach to financial maneuverings. In January 2021, stocks in the company increased suddenly from about U.S. $18 dollars a share, to U.S. $347 dollars before coming down to about U.S. $193 dollars. In 2021, investors on the social media news site Reddit collectively caused hedge fund, Melvin Capital, to lose billions of dollars, while at the same time suddenly boosting the price of shares in GameStop.

Generally Accepted Accounting Principles (GAAP) The accounting professions in the United States and Canada have established GAAP as guidelines that are used in financial reporting. The U.S. and Canadian GAAP are not identical. Companies usually state whether they follow U.S. GAAP or Canadian GAAP. Research by Choi and Young (2015) suggests that non-GAAP earnings disclosures tend to be driven by a desire for informative (strategic) reporting when GAAP earnings beat (undershoot) market expectations.

Generally Accepted Auditing Standards (GAAS) are a set of systematic guidelines used by auditors when conducting audits on companies' financial records. GAAS helps to ensure the accuracy, consistency, and verifiability of auditors' actions and reports. The Auditing Standards Board (ASB) of the American Institute of Certified Public Accountants (AICPA) created GAAS and should Certified Public Accountants fail to follow GAAP they can be held in violation of the code of professional ethics. The coronavirus pandemic in 2020 to 2021 made the application of new auditor reporting standards developed by the AICPA's Auditing Standards Board (ASB) difficult for several audit firms to implement. The ASB consequently delayed the effective dates of its issued Statements on Auditing Standards (SASs). Advice on what actions auditors should take is given by Dohrer, Delahanty, and Goldman (2020).

Gilt-Edged Securities (Gilts) are fixed interest securities or stock issued by the British Government in the form of exchequer stocks or treasury stocks. As they are issued by the British Government, they are considered to be a very low investment risk. There are redeemable gilts that are redeemable after 15 years or more; medium gilts are redeemable in 5 to 15 years; and short-dated gilts are redeemable in less than five years. Index-linked gilts were introduced by the British Government in 1981 and a thorough discussion of their impact since that date is given by Oliver and Rutterford (2020).

Going Concern Opinion (GCO): See Audit Opinion.

Goodwill is generally measured as the difference between the value of the separable items of the business and the total value of the business. A study by Knauer and Wöhrmann (2016) examines the information content of goodwill write-downs under International Accounting Standard (IAS36 Impairment of Assets) and Statement of Financial Accounting Standards (SFAS No. 142). They found a negative capital market reaction to announcements of unexpected goodwill write-offs. Their results indicate that investors react more negatively when a country's level of legal protection is low and allows more management discretion. In January 2017, FASB issued *Accounting Standards Update (ASU) 2017-04, Intangibles-Goodwill and Other (Topic 350): Simplifying the Test for Goodwill Impairment*, which eliminated the calculation of implied goodwill fair value. Instead, companies will record an impairment charge based on the excess of a reporting unit's carrying amount of goodwill over its fair value. This guidance simplifies the accounting as compared to prior GAAP. An article by Ayres, Campbell, Chyz, and Shipman (2019) provides an overview of the goodwill impairment assessment under the new guidance and some specific income tax considerations regarding the financial implications of goodwill impairment.

Gray Market is any market for goods that are in short supply. It differs from black markets as gray markets are normally legal where black markets are not. An example of a gray market is where shares have not been issued but will shortly and market makers may decide to deal with investors or speculators who are willing to trade in anticipation of receiving an allotment of these shares or are willing to cover their deals after flotation.

An investor who does not receive an anticipated allotment has to buy the shares in the open market, usually at a loss. Questions frequently arise as to the reasons why gray markets persist in the economy. Autrey, Bova, and Soberman (2015) offer reasons firms might not implement control systems to prevent gray market distribution in sectors where investment spillovers are common (e.g., the technology sector) and, more broadly, the reasons gray markets persist in the economy.

Green Audit is an audit of the possible effect of an organization on the environment. See ESG.

Green Finance Institute is an independent, commercially focused organization established in 2019 as a direct response to a key policy recommendation made by the industry-led Green Finance Taskforce to the UK Government in March 2018. The institute convenes and leads sectoral coalitions of global experts that identify and unlock barriers to investment toward impactful, real-economy outcomes to benefit the environment, society, and business. The declared mission is to accelerate the transition to a clean, resilient, and environmentally sustainable economy by channeling capital at pace and scale toward real-economy outcomes that will create jobs and increase prosperity for all.

Gross Domestic Product (GDP) is a statistical measure of the domestic output of a country. The gross national product (GNP) and the GDP differ in the way in which imports and exports are measured. The GDP provides a comparison with the past performance of a country and comparisons with other countries. The equation for GDP is:

$$\text{GDP} = \text{Consumption} + \text{Investment} + \text{Government expenditures} + \text{Exports} - \text{Imports}.$$

An article by Scholl and Schermuly (2020), which is based on psychological research on the distribution and use of power, predicted that a steeper distribution of power induces more corruption and elaborated its negative consequences in a complex causal model. A different approach was adopted by Sabia (2015) who concluded that difference-in-difference-in-difference estimates suggest that a 10 percent increase in the minimum wage is associated with a short-run 1 to 2 percent decline in state GDP generated by lower-skilled industries relative to more highly skilled industries.

Gross Margin refers to a company's performance with respect to its profitability before taking into account overhead or operating costs. For example, if a company sells goods for total proceeds of $100K and the direct cost of producing (or acquiring) those goods is $60K, then the gross margin is $40K, usually expressed as a percentage, that is, 40 percent G.M. After subtracting fixed (i.e., overhead) expenses such as salaries and rent, from the Gross Margin, the result is Net Profit (before tax). A study by Kesavan, Gaur, and Ananth Raman (2010) concluded that historical inventory and gross margin contain information useful to forecast sales and that equity analysts do not fully utilize this information in their sales forecasts.

H

Harvesting Strategy attempts to make the maximum short-term gain from a particular profit or service prior to withdrawing it from the market. The strategy is implemented by eliminating or reducing as many of the costs as possible. Current marketing costs may be reduced on the assumption that advertising incurred earlier will continue to have an effect and the possibility of manufacturing costs being reduced will be considered. There may be no public announcement of the potential withdrawal of the project from the market place as this may have an adverse effect on sales. There is not much published literature on the subject, but an interesting article by Noailly, van den Bergh, and Withagen (2003) examines the strategies used in managing renewable resources, such as fisheries and forestry. The term "harvesting" is also used in other situations, and Kern (2015) explains in a short and helpful article the practice of tax loss harvesting.

Hedge Funds are high return and relatively high-risk funds in which the risks are hedged through diversification or offsetting investments. Hedge funds attempt to preserve capital while achieving high returns for their investors. The name comes from the fact that they may be used as a "hedge" (i.e., safeguard) against risk. These funds can take long or short positions, invest in commodities, futures, bonds or stocks, buy and sell options, invest in private companies—almost anything where impressive gains could be realized. For example, to protect against a downturn in the market, a fund that holds a basket of stocks could short futures contracts. To hedge against other risks, for example, weather-dependent crop shortfalls, a fund could sell Orange Juice futures as a hedge against inclement weather. Wang, Wu, and Tong (2015) have conducted a useful study into hedging with futures. FASB has issued Accounting Standards Update (ASU) No. 2017-12, Derivatives and Hedging (Topic 815): Targeted Improvements to Accounting for Hedging Activities. It is designed to make hedge accounting easier to apply in addition to making it more reflective of hedging activities and a useful guide to the requirements to the standard is given by Murphy (2020).

Herfindahl – Hirschman Index (HHI) is a lengthy title but is a commonly accepted measure of market concentration. It is calculated by squaring the market share of each firm competing in a market and then summing the resulting numbers. It can range from close to zero to 10,000. The U.S. Department of Justice uses the HHI for evaluating potential mergers issues. A study by Brezina, Pekár, Cicková, and Reiff (2016) proposed an approach of setting boundary ranges to characterize the concentration of the industry, and Kim (2019) used the technique to investigate aid for trade. He concluded that continuous efforts are required to evaluate and monitor aid for trade to improve their effectiveness and to produce the best possible development path for the international community.

Holding Gains occur due to the length of time a company has held an asset and an increase in prices for such an asset. The holding gain is realized when the assets is sold but no gain is realized if the asset continues to be held in the business. In times of inflation, holding gains are illusory because of changes in purchasing power. Marshall and Lennard (2016) examined this issue and considered the items of income and expense that should be reported in other comprehensive income rather than in profit or loss. Research conducted by Dong and Zhang (2018) examined the selective trading of available-for-sale (AFS) securities by U.S. banks after the implementation of fair value accounting under Statement of Financial Accounting Standards No. 115, Accounting Standards Codification Topic 320. Their results indicated that there is earnings management among banks that choose to report unrealized holding gains and losses in the statement of shareholders' equity but not in the income statement.

Hostile Takeover is the position where a corporate takeover attempt is strongly resisted by the target firm. This can result in various consequences including low morale among employees, a situation researched by Unsal and Rayfield (2020). Usually, a hostile takeover attempt is made by a competitor holding the opinion that an acquisition of a company can be at a bargain price or as a method to eliminate competition. This may happen when market conditions are poor and valuation multiples are lower thus making acquisition targets more appealing. A hostile takeover bid may be opposed by directors but shareholders may accept the bid if the price offered is sufficiently high. Kinsella (2017) provided a useful review of the literature on the topic and suggestions of further avenues for research.

Human Resource Accounting is the financial recognition of an organization's employees by calculating factors such as discounted future earnings or market prices. One argument for human resource accounting is that organizations can incur substantial expense in recruiting and training employees. Under current accounting regulations, these costs are charged as an expense but could be regarded as an essential investment. Another argument is that members of professional sporting teams are often acquired and sold at very high amounts. Although the subject attracts some academic interest, there are no suggestions that the practice of human resource accounting should be subject to any accounting regulations. A useful review of the literature has been conducted by Steen and Welch (2011).

Hyperinflation refers to very rapid, out-of-control inflation. There is no exact definition of what constitutes hyperinflation but it is generally agreed that it occurred in Germany in 1922 when the country printed banknotes so liberally that consumers had to take bags full of currency to make purchases. Inflation has been over 100 percent for many countries at various times in their history. Since inflation for stable economies is in the low single digits, it is generally understood that inflation above 10 percent would constitute hyperinflation. There are several articles on specific countries where hyperinflation has been a major problem. A recent article by Hanke, Krus, and Gawlik (2020) examines hyperinflation in Poland during the Second World War. The authors claim that Poland has had more cases of hyperinflation than any other country.

I

Incentive Stock Options are rights given to employees to purchase a specified number of shares in the organization at a specified price during a specified period. A thoughtful article by Cappelli, Conyon, and Almeda (2020) using a social exchange theory approach suggests that broad-based stock options create a social exchange relationship between the employer and employees, leading to higher individual job performance in the next period. A different approach is given by Black (2020) who argues that the associated complexities and lost tax benefits may make incentive stock options more trouble than they are worth.

Income Smoothing is the manipulation of items in an organization's financial statements to reduce significant changes so that a smooth trend can be reported. It is argued that this approach maintains investors' confidence by announcing a steady increase in profits each year. Not surprisingly, this subject has been investigated by a number of academics and Obaidat (2018), using a sample of firms listed on the Amman Stock Exchange (ASE), concluded that the results indicated no significant relationship between the firm's income smoothing and stock market price volatility. A study by Bok, Choi, and Farber (2020) of a large sample of firms concluded that managerial ability is positively related to smoothing and that high-ability managers incorporate more forward-looking information about cash flows into current earnings through smoothing, thereby enhancing earnings information.

Income Statement: See Profit Statement.

Index-Linked Gilt is a security where there is an obligation to increase both interest and redemption payments pro rata in the retail price index. A thoughtful article by Oliver and Rutterford (2020) described the reasons why the UK government introduced index-linked gilts in 1981. The subsequent events indicate that despite early problems, the introduction of inflation-linked bonds in the United Kingdom was deemed a success.

Initial Coin Offerings (ICO) is the process by which entrepreneurial ventures raise funds for the development of blockchain-based businesses. The subject has attracted consider interest, and Masiak, Block, Masiak, Neuenkirch, and Pielen (2020) have provided a comprehensive view of the phenomenon. The perils and dangers are well identified in an article by Cohney, Hofman, Sklarof, and Wishnick (2020).

Initial Public Offering (IPO) is a company's first issues shares to investors. This is the primary market for stocks in which individuals buy shares straight from the company. An IPO is one way for a company to raise the funds necessary to expand business and a high number of IPO's may indicate a growing economy. Companies that believe they can get a good price for their stock are more likely to go public. In order to issue the shares, a company might hire an investment banker to underwrite or purchase the stock and sell it to the public at a higher fee. When doing an IPO, an underwriter, that is, a stockbroker firm, handles the distribution of shares to the public. Effectively, the brokerage firm subscribes (underwrites) for the shares and then sells them to its clients (investors). After the IPO, the shares will then trade on a stock exchange. It is sometime referred to as "going public." Entrepreneurs and VCs (Venture, or "vulture" Capitalists) sometimes call it "cashing in." Until a company is public, it is considered a private company and does not have to make financial disclosures.

Insider Dealing is the action of dealing in securities to make a profit or avoid a loss while having access to price sensitive information. Such information may have been obtained illegally and, if it were made available publicly, the market price of the securities would be affected. Unfortunately, the evidence suggests that insider dealing is taking place in most countries, and Barnes (1996) provided empirical evidence concerning share price performance of both the target and the bidder prior to the public announcement of a merger bid and the inferences that may be made concerning insider dealing. A brief glance at the many very recent articles suggests that insider dealing is still taking place in most countries.

Institute of Chartered Accountants in England and Wales (ICAEW) was established by royal charter in 1880 and has more than 150,000 members. To become an ICAEW Chartered Accountant, it is necessary to achieve the ACA qualification. However, some members of professional accountancy bodies within the European Union are eligible to apply for ICAEW membership under either the Statutory Audit Directive or the Recognition of Professional Qualifications (RPQ) Directive. In 2010, the ICAEW introduced its "Pathways to Membership" program, which allows fully qualified members from certain professional bodies to apply for membership based on their experience.

Intangible Assets have been a topic of considerable discussion for several years and assets such as brands have appeared on the balance sheet of companies. Standard setters have provided guidance on the appropriate treatment but it remains a subject for debate. A useful literature review by Nichita (2019) examined all categories of intangibles, both recognized and not recognized, in accounting research papers over 19 years. A more recent article by Baranes (2020) covers the framework of intangible assets within the business enterprise from a Veblen-Commons perspective.

Integrated Reporting has developed due to the needs of various groups, including the general public, who wishing to understand how an organization operates. The expansion in the amount of information disclosed can be confusing. The links between the different elements need to be made clear, and the International Integrated Reporting Council (IIRC) was formed in 2010. Their interest is on businesses' value creation, and its aim is to be the next step in the evolution of corporate reporting. It states its mission is to create the globally accepted Integrated Reporting Framework that elicits from organizations information about their strategy, governance, performance, and prospects in a clear, concise, and comparable format. It sets out a number of requirements that are to be applied before an integrated report can be said to be in accordance with the Integrated Reporting Framework. However, from the research they have conducted, Slack and Cambell (2016) concluded that although there is some use of and familiarity with Integrated Reporting, it appears to be limited and that there is little evidence of either use of or demand for Integrated Reporting among many mainstream fund managers or sell-side analysts. At this stage, it is difficult to measure the extent of information provided by companies and its use by recipients of Integrated Reporting. A guide to the stage of development in the United States can be found on the following website: https://iruscommunity.org/directory-united-states-integrated-reports. A review of the progress of Integrated Reporting can be found on https://drcaroladams. net/evidence-of-the-take-up-of-integrated-reporting/. Needless to say, all the large firms of accountants have a substantial amount of information on the subject on their websites.

Intellectual Property can take the form of an asset if it is the result of invention, generation, or ownership of items that provide financial benefits. Such items would be trademarks, patents, logos, and similar items that will result in future economic benefits. Such items, if they meet the requirements of applicable legislation, can appear in the financial statements of an organization. The subject raises several problems in relation to disclosures. Intellectual property could be regarded as a trade secret and the owner has little enthusiasm for significant disclosures. A very thorough study of venture capital, intellectual property rights, and innovation has been made by Safari (2017). There is also the problem that concepts and attitudes in different countries do not lend themselves to disclosures on intellectual property. An insightful article by Mandel, Olson, and Fast (2020) explores cross-cultural differences between American and Chinese attitudes toward intellectual property rights, personal property rights, and real property rights.

Interest Cover is a ratio that is used to determine the financial strength of an organization. It is calculated by identifying the number of times interest charges are covered by earnings before interest and tax. The ratio is used to determine the impact on an organization to changes in interest rates or profit fluctuations. If an organization has a low interest cover ratio, it suggests that it may not be able to pay a dividend to its shareholders.

It is a useful ratio that can be very informative and is easy to calculate. The purpose of the ratio is to determine the number of times the current interest charges can be paid out of current profits before interest and tax. Instead of PBIT, you may see the acronym EBIT meaning earnings before interest and tax.

$$\frac{\text{Profit}\left(\text{earnings}\right)\text{ before interest and tax}}{\text{Interest charge}} = \text{Number of times.}$$

If the interest charge can be paid, that is, is covered, several times from the organization's profit, investors can be confident that they will receive their financial payout. Lenders will receive their interest and existing shareholders should receive some form of dividend. In an economic downturn the low leveraged company is less risky than a highly leveraged company. With a highly leveraged company, the number of times that profits can cover interest charges will be very few. If the profits are insufficient to cover the interest charges, the company is insolvent. In the worst situation, if there are insufficient profits to cover interest, there is the possibility that the company will go into bankruptcy. When the economy is booming, profits are higher and a company can pay its interest charges and a dividend. The lower the interest cover, the weaker the company's financial position looks. If the company can only pay its interest, shareholders will not receive a dividend. If the interest falls below 1.0, lenders are not going to receive all the interest they are due in that financial period. The company has significant financial problems, and it is probable that it will not be able to continue without taking some major actions.

Interest Rate Swaps is where two parties agree to pay the interest of the other party for a specified length of time. It is usual for a fixed rate of interest to be exchanged for a floating rate. Usually, each party must pay the interest on their own loans and subsequently the difference in the interest charges is settled between themselves. A well-researched article is by Benos, Payne, and Vasios (2020).

Internal Controls are the procedures and systems used by an organization to ensure efficient operations and to avoid fraud or misconduct. The system should ensure that management policies are maintained, assets are safeguarded, and the records maintained by the organization are both complete and accurate. Normally, internal audits will be conducted to ensure that all the controls are effective. A thorough study by Lobo, Wan, Yu, and Zhao (2020) examined the association between material weakness in internal controls disclosed under Section 302 of the Sarbanes–Oxley Act of 2002 (SOX) and future stock price crash risk. They concluded that relative to firms with effective internal controls, firms with material weakness have lower financial reporting precision.

Internal Rate of Return (IRR) is the annualized rate of return (in percent) of an investment using compound interest rate calculations. These are frequently part of many time-value-of-money programs, including the financial functions in popular spreadsheets such as 1-2-3 and Excel as well as many calculators and online web-based calculators. A brief but useful article by Carlton Collins (2017) explains the three functions on Excel for calculating the internal rate of return. The IRR is calculated at the point when the NPV of cash outflows (the cost of the investment) and cash inflows (returns on the investment) equal zero. An unusual but interesting study that involved the Internal Rate of Return used the Norwegian population panel data with nearly career-long earnings histories to demonstrate the causal relationship between schooling and earnings over the life cycle (Bhuller, Mogstad, and Salvanes 2017).

International Accounting Standards Board (IASB) was formally the International Accounting Standards Committee founded in 1973 by the accountancy bodies, not the governments, of nine countries: Australia, Canada, France, Germany, Japan, Mexico, the Netherlands, the United Kingdom and Ireland (UK), and the United States. It was established as a private sector nongovernment organization (NGO) with a part-time body of standard setters who met three or four times a year in cities around the globe. The organization was based in London, UK, with a small, full-time secretariat. After several years, the IASC was succeeded by the IASB. This body retained all the IASs that had been issued. It also continues to issue regulations but named them International Financial Reporting Standards (IFRSs. It commenced with IFRS 1 First Time Adoption of International Financial Reporting Standards and in 2016 issued IFRS 16 Leases. A nontechnical guide to the standards that have been issued is given by Hussey and Ong (2020).

International Ethics Standards Board for Accountants (IESBA) is a global independent standard-setting board. The IESBA's mission is to serve the public interest by setting ethics standards, including auditor independence requirements. It aims to raise the bar for ethical conduct and practice for all professional accountants PAs worldwide through a robust, globally operable *Handbook of the Code of Ethics for Professional Accountants*. Its objective is to issue high-quality, internationally appropriate ethics standards for professional accountants, including auditor independence requirements. It launched its Code in June 2019 to help PAs better understand and applied the revised and restructured International Code of Ethics for Professional Accountants (including the International Independence Standards). Pieters (2019) explains some of the key features of the eCode and describes how technology is being used to improve access to and use of professional standards.

Inventory Turnover is an efficiency ratio that measures the average number of times stock has been sold and replaced during the year. There is the reasonable assumption that quick stock turnover is the mark of an efficient company and also a strong demand for its output. The turnover rate will depend on the type of product and the nature of the industry. What reflects an inefficient management is when the factory is continuing with full production and the sales team cannot find customers. The formula for the ratio is:

$$\frac{\text{Cost of sales}}{\text{Average inventory}}.$$

The profit and loss account should allow the amounts for the average inventory to be calculated. If a figure for opening stock is not provided, you can use closing stock for the previous year as the proxy, and the following formula can be used:

$$\frac{\text{Opening inventory} + \text{Closing inventory}}{2}.$$

Research by Johnston (2018) examined trends in inventory efficiency based on inventory turnover for U.S. manufacturing firms for several years. The results of the study showed that there has been a level trend between 1980 and 2013 after controlling for firm size.

J

Job Costing, also known as specific-order costing, is an accounting method used by organizations to determine the costs of conducting a one-off activity and control the costs. Jobs are usually identified as a piece of work, carried out to a customer's specific requirements. Whether a quote has to be provided for painting the outside of a domestic residence or for building a bridge across a river, control of costs is essential. The purpose of the method is to "quote" the cost of a job, whether it involves a tangible product or a particular service for a client. The quote is based not only on all the costs for doing the job but also on a measure of profit. This is not usually disclosed to the customer. A company taking on a job can record the direct costs, such as materials and labor, but there are also the overhead costs such as administration, advertising, and depreciation on equipment. Possibly because of its very practical nature, the subject attracts few research studies but most textbooks explain the basics including one by Hussey and Ong (2021).

Joint Venture is a contractual arrangement in which two or more parties jointly control an economic activity. Joint ventures can have many different forms and structures requiring different accounting treatments. A joint venture public–private partnerships (PPPs) allow partners to share in the risks and rewards of joint production. An article by Higgins and Huque (2015) examines joint ventures as PPPs and formulates a comprehensive performance evaluation framework. The case studied is Hong Kong's Disneyland Resort. This was a project that has endured several challenges related to achieving objectives, ensuring cooperation among partners, and upholding principles of democratic accountability. Where there is an international joint venture, there are many specific issues and these have been discussed by Bai, Chang, and Li (2019).

K

Kaizen Costing can be used in manufacturing or the service sector. The basis of the technique is that it encourages everyone in the company to continually reconsider how the task is undertaken and whether there is a better way of doing it. Usually, it concentrates on the production phase and on achieving continuous, incremental improvements over a period of time to reduce costs. The emphasis is on the process of production rather than the product. The principles can be used in the service sector. For example, a hospital may use the technique to reduce waiting times. A useful guide to the literature on the subject is given by Kaur and Kaur (2013).

Key Performance Indicators (KPIs) are operating and other statistical metrics that cover both financial and nonfinancial reporting information. KPIs are based on GAAP information or provide nonfinancial information such as number of stores, number of employees, and number of subscribers or advertisers. As there may be many stakeholder groups with a need to analyze an entity, each of these stakeholder groups may view and analyze the nonprofit activities from a different perspective and will use a different set of KPIs. They are also increasingly being used by companies in their annual financial reports to shareholders. An interesting article on the use of KPIs is given by Haber and Schryver (2017).

Kiting simply explained is fraud. It is conducted by issuing or altering a check or bank draft for which there are insufficient funds to obtain additional credit that is not authorized. A very helpful article by Ilter (2018) concludes that if the accounting treatment is changed both for the banks and the businesses, the possibility of check kiting and misrepresentation of cash balances will end.

Kurtosis is a statistical technique that identifies how heavily the tails of a particular distribution differ from the tails of a normal distribution. Datasets that have heavy tails usually have a high kurtosis and those with low kurtosis have light tails or lack of outliers. A recent article by Chang, Monahan, Vasvari, and Florin (2021) evaluates whether reported accounting numbers are informative about earnings uncertainty and whether earnings uncertainty is priced. The research used quantile regressions to forecast the standard deviation, skewness, and kurtosis of future earnings. A different subject was selected by Sheraz and Dedu (2020) who conducted a statistical analysis of Bitcoin Cash (BCH) in the U.S. dollar using daily Close, Open, Low, and High returns of BCH data series. The monthly divided daily returns study describes further properties such as skewness, kurtosis, and correlation analysis.

L

Leverage Ratios calculate the amount of capital that comes in the form of debt (loans) to assist in assessing the ability of a company to meet its financial obligations. Companies normally rely on a mixture of equity and debt to finance their operations and knowing the amount of debt held by a company is useful in determining whether it can pay off its debts as they come due. A company is regarded as highly leveraged when its long-term funds are significantly higher than those for similar companies and is considered a speculative investment for the ordinary shareholder. Regulations by standards setters can change leverage ratios. Morales-Diaz and Zamora-Ramirez (2018) confirmed previous research that found important systematic impacts on key balance sheet financial ratios (mainly leverage ratios), on a magnitude that depends on the operating lease intensity of the sector in which the entity operates. The most affected sectors are retail, hotels, and transportation.

Lien is where an asset is pledged as security against a loan, the lender is said to take "lien", that is, a legal security interest, in the asset. Liens are usually registered against assets and recorded in a public office (or online). A buyer of an asset should conduct a search to ensure that there are no liens against that asset to prevent it being sold to an unsuspecting buyer in which case the lien holder has a priority interest in the asset. Not surprisingly, the topic of liens attracts many articles from a wide variety of situations. To exemplify this, we note two recent articles, one by Kitts (2020) on maritime liens and the other on employee wage lien law by Levin, Mingione, and Tisman (2019).

Life Cycle Costing calculates the total of all the costs of a product, service, or asset over a defined period of time. The costs include acquisition, installation, operation, production, maintenance, refurbishment, and disposal. The technique is future-orientated and compels managers to examine the long-term financial implications of the strategic decisions they are making. It also encourages managers to examine and question the costs incurred at every significant stage in the entire life of the product. One study by Knauer and Möslang (2018) has found that companies reported that the greatest benefit of life cycle costing is related to the identification of cost drivers. This is critical knowledge if a business is to be managed successfully.

Linear Interpolation is a technique used in the DCF method for project appraisal to calculate the approximate rate of return. The cash flows for the project are discounted at two discount rates to obtain a small negative NPV. It is assumed that there is a linear relationship between the discount rate that would give an NPV of zero. Examples of the use of the technique are focused usually on specific situations and do not provide a general guide to the use of the technique.

Liquidated is where a company is dissolved by selling all of its assets and then using the cash to meet any obligations to creditors. Any remaining cash will then go to the shareholders of the company. Financial Accounting Standards Board (FASB Accounting Standards Update (ASU) requires an entity's management to evaluate the going-concern assumption, stipulate stricter requirements for disclosure of going-concern uncertainties, and address financial reporting requirements if an entity's liquidation becomes imminent. A useful article by Trainor, Phillips, and Cangialosi (2018) argued that there are several issues concerning regulatory proposals. They also observed that the revision of the going-concern standard aligns U.S. GAAP with International Financial Reporting Standards (IFRS) in that both sets of standards emphasize management's responsibility for evaluating and disclosing going-concern uncertainties but differences between GAAP and IFRS still remain.

Liquidity Coverage Ratio is a stress test that aims to anticipate marketwide shocks and make sure that financial institutions possess suitable capital preservation to manage any short-term liquidity disruptions that may influence the market if a security, such as a stock, does not trade actively. This information indicates that investors have an illiquid market and it is difficult to buy or sell stock without a major impact on price. For small cap, and especially micro-cap stocks, liquidity is a very important requirement. It assists in ensuring an orderly, efficient, and fair market.

Du (2017) has conducted a study of U.S. Bank Holding Companies to ascertain firstly the LCR's marginal contribution to a firm's systemic risk and second whether the LCR can predict *ex ante* that banks are most exposed to systemic losses in a true systemic event.

M

Management Accounting came many years after financial accounting, but it does have a lengthy history starting with the title "cost accounting". If we consider the United Kingdom, a form of management accounting can be traced from the later Middle Ages (Boyns and Edwards 1997). It is suggested that the nature of the disciple changed in the 1970s because of the scale and nature of the changes in management accounting theories and practices. Pelz (2019) conducted a thorough systematic literature search and concluded that the term refers mainly to business planning, accounting-based management control activities, and financial accounting.

Margin Calls can arise where an investor and a broker have invested equal amounts in securities. As the stock price rises and falls, the invested amount changes in value. There is a maintenance margin, as a percentage, of the minimum amount of the investor's equity that should be in the account. A margin call is usually made when the investment is below a certain amount, known as the maintenance margin that is usually expressed as a percentage. A margin call requires the investor to choose either to deposit more funds in the account or to sell some of the assets held in the account. Dou, Masulis, and Zein (2019) in a substantial study researched the pledging of company stock by insiders as collateral for personal bank loans. They found that margin calls triggered by severe price falls exacerbate the crash risk of pledging firms and since margin calls may cause insiders to suffer personal liquidity shocks or to forgo private benefits of control, they also found that it is associated with reduced firm risk-taking.

Medium of Exchange refers to any item that can be used to exchange for goods or services. Originally, many different items were used including salt but this presented problems, and William and Hansen (2013) have explained the move to the use of coins commencing in Sumeria. Government officials commenced using clay tokens of various geometric shapes and patterns with one token equaling one measure of grain. Gradually standard coinage developed with Europe leading to goods being assigned a monetary value. Instead of an account being recorded in units of wheat, the cost of wheat, expressed in a currency, was now recorded. However, currencies are subject to change and Taggart (1953) points to the concept of measurement using the assumption of a stable homogenous dollar as a measuring unit raises problems as the amount identified does not have the same purchasing power over time. Different types of money are now recognized as mediums of exchange including commodity money, representative money, the new cryptocurrency, and fiat money frequently appearing in digital form as well as physical tokens such as coins and notes.

MeMe Stock is simply a stock when the share price of a company is pushed significantly up by individual investors. These are often users of Reddit and Robinhood and the stocks that are shorted are generally ones with single digit prices.

Merger and Acquisition refers to the buying and selling of businesses by merging them with an existing one or simply having one firm acquiring another firm. There are many articles examining mergers and acquisitions in different countries and internationally. Nearly all published research has been directed at manufacturing and service companies, but Sinkin and Putney (2017) have conducted various projects. In one study, they concluded that the mergers of accounting firms are a typical way for accounting firms to grow, expand into new markets, build expertise, and provide for succession.

Money Laundering is the practice of converting money from illegal sources into an apparently legitimate source. It is not always money and cash purchases of high-value goods are also used. There is a concentrated legislative attempt to reduce such activities and accountants and other professionals have been encouraged to report any suspicions involving clients. The Panama Papers in 2015 was the world's largest whistleblower case that involved 11.5 million leaked documents and over 214,000 offshore entities all linked back to one Panamanian law firm. An interesting article by Del Mundo (2019) reviewed the global responses to the Panama Papers, the proposed reforms and strategies, and the obstacles to moving forward.

Monte Carlo Simulation Model (MCSM) is sometimes applied to any technique that approximates solutions to quantitative problems through statistical sampling. The method calculates results each time using a different set of random values from the probability functions. The technique depends on the process of explicitly representing uncertainties by specifying inputs as probability distributions. If the inputs describing a system are uncertain, the prediction of future performance is necessarily uncertain. Ammar, Annabi, Sim, and Wright (2020) conducted a relevant study using a Monte Carlo Simulation Model to measure corporate dividend risk.

N

National Association of Securities Dealers Automated Quotation (NASDAQ) is the major electronic stock exchange in the United States and has a large number of technology companies listed. It is a highly regulated market with strict reporting and compliance regulations that companies must meet. If listed companies fail to meet these standards or fail to comply, they risk being delisted. The NASDAQ100 is an index of 100 technology stocks that trade on the Nasdaq Stock Exchange. NASDAQ is a competitor of the New York Exchange, and in a well-researched study, Bui, Chance, and Stephens (2019) concluded that the two exchanges have reached a stage in their evolution in which a transfer by a company from NYSE to NASDAQ is a virtually immaterial event and seems to occur for other reasons.

Net Asset Turnover, also known as Capital Turnover, measures the number of times the net assets been used (i.e., turned over) during the year to achieve the sales revenue. Generally, the more frequently the net assets are "turned over," the more successful is the business. The capital employed total is usually used to measure net assets. The ratio is expressed as the number of times rather than a percentage and the formula is:

$$\frac{\text{Turnover}}{\text{Capital employed}}.$$

Some research studies have used the total assets instead of net assets. Zarb (2016) used this approach to identify that net profit margin, current ratio, total asset turnover, and earnings before tax are statistically significant with respect to earning power in airline companies.

Net Present Value (NPV) is the differences between the present value of cash inflows and cash outflows for a long-term project. A discount rate is applied to the cash flows so that all future-predicted cash flows have present values. The inflows and outflows may be uncertain and the selection of the appropriate discount rate is critical. A project is normally expected to show a return higher than the discount rate. If the NPV is negative, the project is normally rejected on financial grounds, although there may be political and other pressures. As projects have uncertainty with unknown probabilities, there are issues and these are addressed in an article by Gaspars-Wieloch (2109) who suggests a procedure that can be used even in the case of asymmetric distributions of net cash flows at particular periods since it considers the frequency of each value. An interesting study by Tuin (2020) using NPV as a measure considers process plant start-up and the critical transition from the project phase to business operation.

Net Profit Margin is the profit before interest and tax expressed as a percentage of the sales figure. This ratio measures the percentage return on sales. The formula is:

$$\frac{\text{Profit before interest and tax}}{\text{Turnover}} \times 100.$$

A study by Prober, Meric, and Meric (2016) using several measures compared the financial characteristics of U.S. and UK manufacturing firms and concluded, amongst other matters, that net profit margin is higher in the U.S. firms than in the UK firms.

New York Stock Exchange was founded in 1792 under the Buttonwood Agreement, this being the name of the tree under which 24 merchants agreed to give each other preference in their dealings. It was formally established in 1817 and its present name was adopted in 1983. It has a very informative website and several books are available, the one published by the Exchange is *New York Stock Exchange: The First 200 Years*, 1st edition by James E. Buck (Editor).

Nonfungible Tokens (NFTs) are units of data on a blockchain which is a digital ledger. They are digital files that can hold forms of creative work such as art, audio, videos, items in video games and provide buyers with proof of *ownership* but access to the original file is not restricted to the owner of the NFT. Chow and Zorthian (2021) described the impact of NFTs in the art world and an informative article that described the relationship of NFTs and blockchain is given by Whitaker (2019).

Norwalk Agreement was established in 2002 by the Financial Accounting Standards Board FASB and the International Accounting Standards Board IASB. At the time, it was regarded as a significant move in demonstrating the convergence of the United States with international accounting standards. Although several meetings and projects were undertaken, the United States decided not to converge with international standards. A book on these events has been written by Hussey and Ong (2018), and there is a more recent article by Elam (2020).

Null Hypothesis has attracted several research studies that have adopted this approach as it assumes there is no significant difference between speci-fied populations, and any observed difference is due to sampling or experi-mental error. Two recent articles with lengthy titles but very useful, contents are one by Sriananthakumar (2019) and the other by MacGillivray (2019).

Number of Days' Inventory is a ratio that measures an organization's abilities in inventory management by measuring the average number of days inventory is held. The formula usually applied is:

$$\frac{\text{Number of units of inventory held}}{\text{Usage of units per annum}} \times 365.$$

The number of units held can be taken at either the start or end of the year or an average of both. This is an internal company ratio but investors with access only to the published financial accounts may use a similar ratio as follows:

$$\frac{\text{Value of inventory}}{\text{Revenue or cost of sales per annum}} \times 365.$$

An article by Kaushik and Chauhan (2019) uses the ratio and examines the relationship between working capital management and firm perfor-mance of Indian firms for the period 2008 to 2016.

O

Off-Balance Sheet Debt is a method for funding an organization's activities without revealing all the finance and corresponding assets on the balance sheet. This results in accounting ratios, such as the leverage ratio, giving a more optimistic picture of finances than may be the true position. One common method of such financing was to create a subsidiary that was so structured that its results were not included in the consolidated accounts. Most regulatory regimes have introduced legislation to prevent, or at least reduce the practice. Sengupta and Wang (2011) examined whether the public debt market prices information on off-balance sheet debt arising from operating leases and postretirement plans, and a study by Kraft (2015) examined a dataset of both quantitative (hard) adjustments to firms' reported U.S. GAAP financial statement numbers and qualitative (soft) adjustments to firms' credit ratings that Moody's develops and uses in its credit rating process.

Opportunity Cost is the benefit or income forgone due to the selection of one specific alternative rather than another when resources are limited or when normally exclusive projects are involved. For example, the opportunity of making one specific product is the revenue gone for the inability to continue the production of another product. Opportunity cost is an important concept in decision making particularly in a situation in which a choice needs to be made between several mutually exclusive alternatives given limited resources. Although it is usually assumed that opportunity costs are underestimated, thus leading to a wrong decision, Weiss and Kivetz (2019) argue that in situations where the need to choose arises from external rather than internal constraints, opportunity costs may actually be overestimated. An unusual study by Blaywais and Rosenboim (2019) examines how cognitive load, being the mental effort invested in decision-making, affects that decision making. Their study showed that the tendency to ignore opportunity costs is stronger under a greater cognitive load and cognitive load causes participants to invest fewer cognitive efforts in choice tasks and take more risks.

Options are contracts that give the right, but not the obligation to buy or sell a fixed quantity of a commodity, security, or currency at a particular date at a particular price, known as the exercise or strike price. The purchaser of the option pays a premium for the option to the seller of the contract to compensate the risk of the seller for payment. The premium is normally nonrefundable. As one would expect, this subject has attracted the attention of many researchers and the following two recent articles add to the literature, one by Lowry, Rossi, and Zhu (2019) and the other by Hiemann (2020). A certain level of understanding of the subject is required to benefit from reading the many articles that have been published.

Out of the Money Options have a strike price which the underlying security has yet to reach so the option has no intrinsic value. There are differences between a call option and a put option depending on whether the strike price is above or below the underlying price. With a call option, if the underlying price is below the strike price, it is an out of the money option. With a put option, where the underlying price is above the strike price, that option is an out of the money option. This topic is of considerable interest to researchers and investors and there are many articles on the topic. We recommend that readers have some knowledge of the subject before tackling the often very technical published articles.

Outsourcing refers to a company buying services from another firm. For example, if company X is outsourcing its e-commerce services, it means that it is relying on another company to do this task rather than doing it internally with its own employees and resources. Many companies outsource much of their production to other countries where the labor costs can be lower and the taxation is also lower than in their home country. There are numerous articles discussing outsourcing in various industries, countries, and situations. The outsourcing of information technology is a very active market and the possible benefits to the client are reviewed by Susarla and Mukhopadhyay (2019).

Overdraft is a deficiency caused by drawing on funds (e.g., in a bank account) causing a default position. If you write a check on your bank account that exceeds the cash in the account, your account will be in an overdraft position if your bank has honored the check. Many bank customers have overdraft privileges. Without such privileges, banks will not allow deficit positions and will return the checks to the payee marked, NSF that is, Not Sufficient Funds (a comfortable way of saying that they "bounced" the check). One study by Ashton and Gregoriou (2017) conducted an analysis using a UK dataset of 222 personal current accounts, recorded monthly between 1995 and 2011, in combination with interest rates from 1,200 instant-access deposit accounts offered contemporaneously by the same firms. Their results showed that personal current accounts offering overdraft facilities have higher deposit and payment service costs than accounts not offering this service.

Overtrading is where an organization has a large growth in operations but not the long-term finance to support this growth and financial support is required for the acquisition of raw materials, and Work-In-Process (WIP). Although short-term strategies, such as delaying payments, and hastening collection of money can provide temporary relief, such strategies do not provide a long-term solution. Overtrading is a particular problem for small organizations in high growth sectors where there may be difficulties in obtaining long-term funding. It can also occur where an economy is emerging from recession thus creating a demand for its products but appropriate financial support is not available. A somewhat dated but useful article that considers the issues and suggests some solutions is by Claye (2000).

P

Par Value is the stated face value of a bond or, in the case of stock, an amount assigned by the company and expressed as a dollar amount per share. Par value of common stock usually has no relationship to the current market value and so no-par value stock is issued. Par value of preferred stock is significant, however, as it indicates the dollar amount of assets each preferred share would be entitled to in the event of liquidation of the company. The issue of par values has not received much research attention but a very thoughtful article by Pennacchi, Vermaelen, and Wolff (2014) on call option enhanced reverse convertible (COERC) incorporates the subject.

Preferred Shares issued by a company have specified rights and privileges. Preferred usually means that the shares are ranked above common shares with respect to payout or dividend rights. They generally also carry an interest rate payment obligation by the company. Preferred shares are considered are less risky and more secure than other types of shares. There is usually less upside potential (unless they are convertible into common shares) associated with them. Smith (2016) has written a useful article on the merits and downsides of preferred shares.

Present Value (or Present Worth) is usually defined as the value of future cash flows discounted to a present value by using an appropriate interest rate. Although the actual calculation of using an appropriate interest rate can usually be easily decided, a reliable calculation of future cash flows can present some problems. This can be resolved by using an "end-of-period convention." With this approach, positive cash flows (i.e., cash inflows) and negative cash flows (i.e., cash outflows) taking place during a financial period are aggregated to the end of the period and their sum, the "net cash flow," is discounted. An article by Dulk (2016) discusses the errors attributable to employing the end-of-period convention to an asset that has both positive and negative cash flows.

Price/Earnings Ratio (P/E) compares the current share price to the previous 12-months' earnings. An example would be where a company had earning $0.50 per share in the previous year. If the share is currently trading at $10.00 per share has a P/E of 20. If you buy a share today and the performance stays the same, you may expect to earn $0.50 on each share you own based on the P/E ratio. High P/E's are common in high tech because of the rapid growth anticipated in future earnings. Technology company P/E's are generally in the 30+ range. Frequently, tech companies do not pay dividends but reinvest the cash to make the company more valuable resulting, hopefully, in the share price going up. The term diluted EPS is used to include such additional shares. An article by Nezlobin, Rajan, and Reichelstein (2016) examined the structural properties of a firm's price-to-earnings (P/E) and price-to-book (P/B) ratios and the relation between these two ratios.

Price–Earnings–Growth Ratio (PEG) compares a company's price-to-earnings multiple to its earnings growth rate. It is calculated by dividing the P/E ratio as explained in the previous entry by the percentage growth rate in earnings. A company with a P/E of 50 and an earnings growth rate of 25 percent has a PEG of 2. Jiang and Kang (2020) discussed the information content of PEG ratios (price/earnings to growth ratios) for future aggregate returns and economic fundamentals. The authors establish an analytic link between PEG ratios and time-varying expected returns of stocks. The link is then combined with empirical asset pricing models to extract marketwide information from cross-sectional PEG ratios. The resultant cross-section estimates of the risk premiums on stock betas serve as proxies for marketwide information. The proxies contain salient information about future market equity premiums and macroeconomic activity both in-sample and out-of-sample. Moreover, the proxies outperform aggregate PEG ratios and the cross-section.

Private Company is a company with a small number of shareholders (less than 50 in some jurisdictions) and is not required to disclose its business affairs to the public. Some government departments, such as the Taxation Department (federal) and the Securities Commission (provincial), use different definitions for "private company." The Private Company Council (PCC) employs a decision-making framework that considers the needs of private company financial statement users as it advises on both possible private company alternatives within GAAP and on impacts to private companies for those items under FASB's active consideration. As an advisory group, the PCC researches the benefits and potential consequences of providing private companies with modified pathways of applying GAAP. Private company stakeholders' perspectives on whether GAAP requirements are useful to drive these alternatives within the context of the decision-making framework. The PCC provides FASB with ongoing advice for projects on the board's agenda. Herron, Herbold, and Reisig (2019) in an article discussed the position of private companies and advised that proposals were open for public comment and are available on the board's website at fasb.org.

Process Costing is a method normally used where the manufacturing is a continuous production process with a large number of identical items. The costs are accumulated for the entire process and averaged over a large number of production units. In some organizations, there may be more than one final product. For example, a company may make a standard model and add something to it so that it also has a "superior model" for sale at a higher price. Despite the importance of this costing method, it appears to have failed to capture the interest of academic researchers.

Profit Margin refers to a company's performance with respect to its net profitability after taking into account overhead or operating costs. A gross profit margin can be calculated and also a net profit margin by subtracting fixed (i.e., overhead) expenses, such as salaries and rent, from the gross margin. An article by Ertan, Lewellen, and Thomas (2020) provides an incisive examination of profit margins and concludes that scale generates margin expansion but that benefit is offset by other effects that reduce margins.

Profit or Loss Account: See Profit Statement.

Profit Statement is sometimes known as the Profit or Loss Account in the UK. In the United States, the terms "Earnings" or "Income Statement" is preferred. The terminology used on the Profit or Income Statement can vary depending on the country and the accounting standards with which it is complying. Even with countries applying International

Accounting Standard, there can be variations in the terms and methods used. It has been argued that it is "unrealistic for a single set of standards to be accepted and implemented in a uniform manner in several different countries to produce innately comparable financial statements" (Ward and Lowe 2017). However, the International Accounting Standards Board continues to issue and improve its financial reporting requirements, which should result in greater comparability.

Prospectus is a formal, legal document in which a company make substantial information disclosures publicly available. It is a formal document about the past, present, and future plans of the company. It is used when raising money from the public to make sure that investors fully understand where and why they are making their investment. If a company makes misleading statements, investors can seek recourse through litigation. It has become more usual for ordinary initial public offerings IPOs to contain going concern opinions. An interesting and timely article by Matanova, Steigner, Yi, and Zheng, (2019) examined this practice.

Pump and Dump denoting the fraudulent practice of encouraging investors to buy shares in a company in order to inflate the price artificially and then selling one's own shares while the price is high. The extent of this practice is not known but insights into the issue and differing opinions are provided in articles by Bebchuk, Brav, and Wei (2015) and Siering (2019).

Put Options is an option to sell an asset or a financial instrument. The parties enter into a contract where it is expected that the price of specific shares will fall. The subject has attracted the interests of several researchers. Two examples that focus on the United States are Du, Xue, and Liu (2019) and Zhu, He, and Lu (2018).

Q

Qualified Opinion is an audit report where the auditor has made a qualification of the financial statements. This could arise from such circumstances as an inappropriate accounting treatment or the accounting treatment does not comply with accounting standards. It is the responsibility of the auditors to ensure that their report reliably reflect the true financial situation of the company. The topic has attracted several research studies, and Sanchez-Medina, Blazquez-Santana, and Alonso (2019) analyzed the effect of the normative change that took place in Spain in December 2010.

Quick Ratio, also known as liquidity ratio or acid-test ratio, is a robust test of an organization's solvency. It is calculated by comparing the liquid assets (current assets less inventory) to the current liabilities.

Quick ratio = (Total Current Assets – Inventory) / Current Liabilities

A ratio above 1 indicates that a business has enough cash to cover its short-term financial obligations and sustain its operations. If the ratio suggests that the company is unable to meet its current liabilities if it were required to do so, the company may find it difficult to find other sources of finance to remedy the position. Although there is no substantial research in this area, a recent article by Tang, Srivastava, Liu, and Farouk (2020) has conducted a study into small and medium-sized enterprises.

R

Random Walk Theory states that share price movements have no predictable pattern and that it is unwise to extrapolate from previous movements. This is the opposite view to chartists who rely on past patterns of movement to predict future prices. In recent years, there has been little research interest in the theory, but a well-referenced article by Peterson, Ma, and Ritchey (1992) explains the earlier debates.

Rate of Return is the gain or economic benefit earned from the investment of resources in a commercial other economic activity. The return is calculated by comparing it to the amount of the investment in some way, usually in percentage terms. The return from an investment in a division or subsidiary may be expressed as an accounting rate of return (ARR) or return on assets. Klebanov (2019) developed a systematic approach to studying rates of return of investments in situations where exact timing of transactions is not known. A different dimension to the discussions has been taken by Das, Kuhnen, and Nagel (2020). They took a sample of more than 180,000 responses from participants in the Michigan Survey of Consumers each month from 1978 to 2014. Their analysis demonstrated that socioeconomic status has a strong influence on individuals' beliefs about future macroeconomic conditions, such as changes in unemployment, business conditions in general, and stock market performance.

Real Rate of Interest is the rate of interest charged on loans or other investments after adjusting for the effects of inflation. For example, if the rate of interest charged for borrowed loans is 6 percent and the inflation rate is 2 percent per annum, the real rate of interest is 4 percent. If the economy has a very high rate of inflation, the adjusted rate of interest may be a negative figure. Abel and Lehmann (2019) argued that there are several problems with this approach and suggested a refocusing of contemporary monetary policy and related theories.

Receivership is a consequence of a company confronting its financial issues but being unable to meet its payment obligations to its creditors. In these circumstances, the company can be placed into "receivership" by the courts. This means that a court-appointed receiver, which is usually a well-known accounting firm, will manage the affairs of the company for an interim period of time during which the receiver will consider proposals from various stakeholders to rescue the company. During this period, the company is allowed to continue doing business, albeit with certain restrictions. Some companies will emerge from receivership and prosper while others may simply be liquidated. An article by Kelly (2019) discussing the role of the SEC in the United States suggest that the SEC can provide the framework for a more efficient system to equitably compensate all defrauded claimants in and out of bankruptcy.

Related Party Transactions (RPTs) are the transfer of assets, liabilities, or the performance of services by, to, or for a related party regardless of whether a price is charged. Hope and Lu (2020) investigated the economic consequences of a 2006 Securities and Exchange Commission (SEC) regulation that mandated public firms to disclose their governance policies on RPTs. They found that the initiation of RPTs significantly reduces the occurrence of RPTs, and that the reduction in RPTs is negatively associated with the implied cost of capital (ICC).

Residual Income is the dollar amount equal to the operating income of a business unit less a charge for the investment in the unit. Residual income is used as a performance measure when evaluating the performance of profit and investment centers and is an alternative to the return on investment ratio. It is argued that residual income ratio is preferable to the return on investment ratio because it encourages managers to accept investment opportunities that have a greater rate of return than the charge for invested capital. Ho, Lee, Lin, and Yu (2017) have compared the reliability of the dividend (DIV) model, the residual income valuation (CT and GLS) model, and the abnormal earnings growth (OJ) model. They concluded that the OJ model yields more reliable estimates.

Return on Capital Employed (ROCE) is a widely used ratio with the term "return" usually meaning Profit Before Interest and Tax (PBIT). Larger companies may identify this as operating profit or Earnings Before

Interest and Tax (EBIT), and smaller companies may use the terms net profit or net earnings. The capital employed is the investment made in the business and this is usually identified as the total invested by shareholders. The ROCE measures the percentage return on the total investment of funds in the business. This demonstrates management's effectiveness in the amount of profit they can generate on the funds over which they have control. ROCE should reflect the element of risk in the investment and can be compared with interest rates for other investments where there is a very small risk of losing money. An interesting study by Hoang, Przychodzen, Przychodzen, and Segbotangni (2020) applied this ratio with others in a study investigating the relationship between environmental performance and financial performance on a sample of 361 U.S. firms over the 2007 to 2016 period.

Rights Issue is a method by which quoted companies can raise more capital by offering existing shareholders the right to purchase stock/shares in proportion to their current holding. As rights are usually issued at a discount to the market price of existing stocks, those not wishing to exercise their rights can sell them on the market. Holderness (2019) in a global assessment of stock holders' rights identifies such stock issues as the most far-reaching issue raised by his research as it encourages management to consult more often with large shareholders, which has the potential to create a more sophisticated shareholder base and ultimately change the dynamics of corporate decision making.

S

Sarbanes-Oxley Act (SOX) is a law the U.S. Congress passed on July 30, 2002 to help protect investors from fraudulent financial reporting by corporations. Also known as the SOX Act of 2002 and the Corporate Responsibility Act of 2002, it mandated strict reforms to existing securities regulations and imposed tough new penalties on lawbreakers. The Act came in response to financial scandals in the early 2000s involving publicly traded companies such as Enron Corporation, Tyco International, and WorldCom. The high-profile frauds shook investor confidence in the trustworthiness and credibility of corporate financial statements and led many to demand an overhaul of decades-old regulatory standards. Understandably, the Act attracted substantial comment and opinion, and Wilbanks (2016) wrote a short and useful article.

Securities and Exchange Commission (SEC) was an outcome of the U.S. stock market crashed in 1929, and it is argued due to poor economic intelligence (Galbraith 2009). This led to the Securities Act in 1933 followed by the establishment of the Securities commission in 1939. The SEC requires public companies to disclose meaningful financial and other information to the public. Although the focus is on public companies, the standards it sets are regarded as good accounting and influences the activities of private companies. The SEC is a very large and powerful organization. Each year civil enforcement actions against individuals for the violation of securities laws and against individuals and companies are taken. The SEC requires certain companies and individuals to file formal financial documents on Form 10k, which is a public document. The SEC does not establish financial regulations, and this is the responsibility of the Financial Accounting Standard Board.

Shares: See Stocks.

System for Electronic Document Analysis and Retrieval (SEDAR) is the Canadian depository for public corporate records. Before the Internet, companies had to report regularly to securities commissions across Canada. Now, they all file with SEDAR, and SEDAR makes all these filings available to the public via the SEDAR website: www.sedar.com.

Share-Based payments are transaction where the entity transfers equity instruments (e.g., shares or share options) in exchange for goods or services supplied by employees or third parties. *Accounting Standards Update No. 2017-09, Compensation - Stock Compensation (Topic 718): Scope of Modification Accounting*, provides guidance on which changes to the terms or conditions of these awards require an entity to apply modification accounting. Previous confusion arose from the term "modification", and the FASB defines it as a change in any of the terms or conditions of a share-based payment award. In addition to reducing diversity in practice, the standard is designed to lower costs and complexity for entities when they apply the guidance in *Topic 718*. The standard is effective for all entities for annual periods that begin after December 15, 2017, and for interim periods within those annual periods. FASB has issued many statements regarding the requirements of the standards and the main accounting journals publish frequent updates and comments.

Share/Stock Buyback or Share/Stock Repurchase is the situation where an entity purchases its own shares, thus reducing the number of shares on the open market. Such an action has repercussions, and a research by Stunda (2017) found that investors perceive earnings associated with nonbuyback firms to be informative and good indicators of stock prices and have a strong correlation with long-term investment. The research study also revealed that investors perceive earnings associated with buyback firms to be "noisy" with unclear indicators of stock prices and not possessing a strong correlation with long-term investment.

Short Selling (Shorting) is any transaction used by an investor to profit from the decline in price of a borrowed asset or financial instrument. Kelley and Tetlock (2017) took a substantial sample of retail trading and found that short selling is a strong predictor of negative stock returns, even after controlling for other traders' behavior and known predictors of returns. They concluded that their findings are consistent with the theory that retail short sellers possess and act on unique information about stocks' fundamental values. Prices gradually incorporate this information within a year.

Special-Purpose Acquisition Company (SPAC) is a publicly traded company that has no commercial operations but has cash that is used to buy private companies and take them public. The first SPAC was listed on the New York Stock Exchange in May 2017 but there are now many more. A useful article by Donahue, Letalien, and Soares (2020) explains the corporate and securities law issues but others consider that SPACs will have a short life (Haverstock and Sergei 2020).

Stagflation was identified in the 1970s and it combines the economic effects of "inflation" (i.e., escalating prices) and "stagnation" (i.e., stagnant) or no economic growth in terms of GDP. Prices as measured by the consumer price index (CPI) may be increasing while the economy is not expanding. When an economy is not growing (stagnant), but prices are increasing, this is not a healthy situation for a country. There are numerous articles on stagnation in several countries and these range from the oil industry, car makers, employees' wages, directors' salaries, unemployment, governments, and any other factor one can offer. The relationship of social benefits and stagflation in the United States has been researched by Lia and Lin (2016). Recent literature has moved slightly from identifying the possible causes originally and suggested that we may experience it again.

Standard Costing establishes the costs to be incurred for various activities. It is used to provide managers with a reporting method and to provide control over actual costs. The organization determines planned levels of expenditure and income, and the actual costs are recorded. The difference between what has been planned and what was achieved is a variance that requires investigation to determine the reasons for the difference. Standard costing is usually used for individual products and processes and is frequently used in manufacturing. An interesting paper by Kulesza, Weaver, Friedman, and Frederick (2011) details the growth of management accounting in methods such as standard costing and activity-based costing. McBride, Hines, and Craig (2016) argued that the method can be traced back to the British Royal Navy many centuries ago.

Statement of Financial Accounting Standards (SFAS) issued in the United States by the Financial Accounting Standards Board have been superseded by the FASB Accounting Standards Codification (ASC).

The codification is effective for interim and annual periods ending after September 15, 2009. All existing accounting standards documents are superseded by the ASC. All other accounting literature not included in the codification is now deemed nonauthoritative.

Stock Exchange is an organization, usually a nongovernment corporation, that manages the trading (i.e., the buying and selling) of shares of companies is called a stock exchange. It provides a market place (i.e., the "stock market") where buyers and sellers trade shares or stocks in corporations. Stock exchanges differentiate themselves by the quality of companies that they list for trading. Some exchanges will list only large, highly valued firms while others, such as junior exchanges, may list fledgling companies looking for speculative investors. In the United States, the stock market crash of 1929 encouraged companies to issue an annual corporate financial report to shareholders and other stakeholders who use it to evaluate financial performance. The Securities and Exchange Commission (SEC) was established in 1934 to remedy the poor corporate information that was available at that time (Galbraith 2009).

Stock Options give company employees the right to buy shares at a certain price (usually the trading price on the date granted) for a certain period of time. If the shares increase, then a handsome profit can be realized at no risk by selling shares at current market prices while at the same time buying shares at below market prices. These are usually called "incentive stock options" and can augment an employee's salary considerably. In many corporations, managers earn far more by exercising stock options than they do by means of a pay check. There are also trading options. These are created in the marketplace between buyers and sellers. There are both CALL options and PUT options and are based on an underlying stock. CALL options allow the holder to buy shares of a company at a particular price for a specified time period. PUT options allow the holder to sell shares of a company at a particular price for a specified time period. Despite the growing interest around the topic, the research is still fragmented and fails to present a comprehensive picture on the factors that affect the aim of stock options. A substantial literature review provides a broad basis by providing a systematization of the studies on the topic (Catuogno, Saggese, Sarto, and Viganò 2016).

Stocks, also referred to as equities or shares, give part ownership in a company. When you buy stocks, you become a company shareholder, giving a claim on part of that company's assets and earnings. The two main types of stocks are common and preferred. If you hold common stock, you can vote at shareholders' meetings and receive dividends. However, you are also at the lowest rank in the corporate ownership structure. Preferred stockholders have a higher claim on assets and earnings than owners of common stock (e.g., they receive their dividends first) but, normally, they would not have voting rights. There are many recent articles on stocks. A novel approach to being up to date with events is an article by Singh and Shaik (2021) entitled *The Short-Term Impact of COVID-19 on Global Stock Market Indices*.

Strategic Cost Management is the application of cost management techniques to simultaneously improve the strategic position of a firm and reduce costs. To understand the character of strategic management, the present company practices are important. Two recent articles providing the details of company practices are by Manapat, Kristoffer, and Sridharan (2020) who relate the method to brand acquisitions and by Wegmann (2019) who considers a four-dimensional typology based on three strategic objectives assigned to the cost accounting systems.

Sustainability Accounting is the term frequently used to include social and environmental accounting, corporate social reporting, corporate social responsibility reporting, or nonfinancial corporate reporting. It is related to the financial statements but connects the companies' strategies from a sustainable framework. It does this by disclosing information on the three levels which are environment, economic, and social. As you can imagine, there is some difficulty in combining these three categories into a format that is easily understood. The Sustainability Accounting Standards Boards (SASB), established in 2011, is the authority on such corporate disclosures. It operates in a governance structure similar to that adopted by other internationally recognized bodies that set standards for disclosure of financial and other types of corporate information. The SASB has a board of directors responsible for the strategy, finances, and operations of the entire organization. There is also a standard-setting board that develops, issues, and maintains the standards. The Board receives no government financing and is not affiliated with any governmental body. In 2018, the SASB published a complete set of 77 industry standards. These identify the set of financially material sustainability topics and their associated metrics for the typical company in an industry. The standards are intended to assist organizations in identifying and communicate opportunities for sustaining long-term value creation. There are numerous articles on the subject and one by Braam and Peeters (2018) focuses, with substantial research data, on the third-party assurance on sustainability reports provided by some companies. The sustainability standards issued by the Sustainability Accounting Standards Boards are available for download on the SASB website at www.sasb.org/.

SWOT Analysis is conducted to identify the strengths, weaknesses, opportunities, and threats of an organization, practice, or process. The analysis can be carried out in a number of different situations including such diverse subjects as international politics and health care. The aim is to assess the current position of the subject of interest at a specific time and the potentials for the future. A recent interesting research study looks at the conditions and prospects for the agricultural sector in Russia during 2018 to 2024, using a SWOT framework (Wegren, Nikulin, and Trotsuk 2019).

Syndicated Loan is a large loan made to the borrower by a group of banks. There is only one loan agreement and the loans are usually made on small margins. Usually, the borrower can reserve the right to know the names of all members of the syndicate. Any change in banking legislation can have an impact on the process (Keil and Muller 2020).

T

Target Costing is a technique that ensures a product is introduced to the market with a specific functionality, quality, and selling price that can be produced at a life-cycle cost to generate an acceptable level of profitability (Cooper and Slagmulder 1999). It is not a complex technique although it requires a change in management thinking and philosophy in a company where the model has always been cost-plus pricing. The possibilities of the value of target costing in even small business have been suggested. The method would involve determining the target price, the target cost, and the target profit. The substantial literature on the subject reveals that target costing is used in several different industries and is not restricted to any one country.

Theory of Constraints is a management approach that focuses on managing bottlenecks or constrained resources by identifying and relaxing the constraints. An extremely thorough analysis of the literature is given by Ikeziri, de Souza, Guptab, and Fiorini (2019) that involved many journal articles published since 1984. Kuruvilla (2018) has pointed out that although it is a tool for convergent thinking and synthesis, the "thinking processes," which underpin the entire theory of constraints methodology, helps to identify and manage constraints and guide continuous improvement and change in organizations.

Total Quality Management is a philosophy rather than a technique. It is assumed that all processes, procedures, and practices can be improved. To bring about these improvements, the technique of TQM encourages employee empowerment. The first stage in implementing TQM is to identify customers and analyze their expectations. Measures are devised to make these expectations achievable in the production process. The measures can be both quantitative (e.g., the time taken for a repair to be conducted) or qualitative (e.g., the image the customer yearns for in buying the product or service). Management and shop floor work together to attempt to bring about the required changes. One must be alert to the possibility that such an approach may lead to major internal disagreements. This subject has attracted a substantial literature and Dahlgaard-Park, with other authors, has published several articles on the topic, a recent one was in 2019.

Trend Analysis endeavors to find whether the amount shown on the financial statements for the present financial period is better or worse than in previous financial periods. Data for several years for particular financial activities or results are either compared to the previous year or over an extended period. This could be weeks, months, or years, if data are available. The method is frequently used to analyze sales and profits but it has a much wider application than that. Watts (2018) applied the technique as part of a study on the emergence and evolution of the biotechnology industry during the 1990s and early 2000s.

Triple Bottom Line was a term introduced by John Elkington (1997), and as the public responsibility of companies became broader, the notion increased in importance. A comprehensive literature review by Vega-Mejía, Montoya-Torres, and Islam (2019) concluded that the distribution or transportation of products are significant components of supply chains' operations and incorporates the "Triple Bottom Line" (TBL) objectives for sustainability, which are the combination of the economic, environmental, and social dimensions. A study by Hussain, Rigoni, and Orij (2018) suggests that theories must try not only to provide rationale for the impact of corporate governance on sustainability but also to explain which dimension of sustainability might be more affected. The authors concluded that the most important implication for practitioners is the support for sustainability practices, which may be gained through implementation of particular corporate governance mechanisms. A more critical approach to the extant literature by Isil and Hernke (2017) concludes that the TBL has evolved into a proxy for sustainability. Using a sentiment analysis, the authors argue that literature views the TBL favorably and uncritically, with only 8 percent of academic studies invoking the term negatively.

U

Under Capitalization is when the financial position of an organization is such that it does not have sufficient capital or reserves for the size of its operations. The position may have been caused unsuspected growth or poor decision making. The organization could be generating healthy profits, but it does not have sufficient cash to pay debts or returns to its shareholders. The result could be bankruptcy. For those interested in the problems of liquidity facing different organizations, a short review of several U.S. cases that were brought to court is given by Weinberger and Murphy (2016).

Unlimited Liability refers to the full legal responsibility that business owners and partners assume for all business debts. This liability is not capped, and obligations can be paid through the seizure and sale of owners' personal assets, which is different than the popular limited liability business structure. A major, but far from recent, case in the United Kingdom (UK). that changed opinion on unlimited liability was that of the City of Glasgow Bank (CGB) in 1878. The events are well explained by Button, Knott, Macmanus, and Willison (2015). They discussed the failure of the bank and the losses that fell entirely on shareholders because they had unlimited liability, which required them to cover any shortfall of assets relative to liabilities. The authors concluded their analysis by arguing that studying the past can help to ensure that historical insights are incorporated into risk assessment and structural policy today.

V

Value Chain Analysis is a strategic method used to evaluate an organization's relationships with suppliers, customers, and competitors. The technique examines the set of interrelated activities needed to design, develop, manufacture, market, and deliver goods or services to customers. The process identifies where in the chain the value to customers can be increased or the costs in each of the activities may be reduced. Krzywdzinski (2017) conducted research that compared labor-use strategies in highly automated automotive supplier plants in a high-wage country (Germany) and a low-wage region (Central Eastern Europe). The study revealed considerable differences regarding skill requirements on the shop floor and the use of precarious employment contracts.

Variable Costing is a decision-making technique that charges only the variable costs to the cost unit and treats the fixed costs as a total amount to be deducted from the total contribution to calculate the profit or loss for the period. Finished goods inventory is valued only on the basis of the variable manufacturing costs and fixed costs are ignored. Another term for this method is direct cost. These costs are usually shown directly under revenues on an income statement as the first costs associated with producing the revenues that are recorded. An article by Herath and Lu (2018) on variable costing explains an approach to detect real earnings management by extracting information from financial statements.

Venture Capital is a form of private equity and a type of financing that investors provide capital to start up companies and small businesses that are believed to have long-term growth potential. Venture capital does not always take a monetary form. It may be in the form of technical or managerial expertise. Venture capital is typically allocated to small companies with exceptional growth potential, or to companies that have grown quickly and appear poised to continue to expand. Though it can be risky for investors who put up funds, the potential for above-average returns is an attractive payoff. For new companies or ventures that have a short operating history, funding is increasingly becoming a popular—even essential—source for raising capital, especially if they lack access to capital markets, bank loans, or other debt instruments. The subject is of considerable interest to academic authors, and an article by Bayar, Chemmanur, and Tian (2020) develops a theoretical model providing a new rationale for venture capitalist.

Vesting refers to stock or stock options that are earned by the holder over time. For example, a company employee may be given stock options that vest over a three-year period. In this case, if the employee quits after one year, only one-third of the options will have been vested and the remainder would be forfeited. Edmans, Fang, and Lewellen (2017) studied the link between real investment decisions and the CEO's short-term stock price concerns.

Volume-Based Cost Driver is a cost driver or activity based that is closely associated with production volumes such as direct labor hours or machine hours. The subject has not attracted significant research interest, but a very useful article by Bilici and Dalci (2008) provides a detailed analysis explaining how the traditional approach to calculating operating leverage factor could lead managers to make irrational or inaccurate profit and production planning decisions. They argue that the theoretical assumptions of activity-based costing can be combined with traditional ones to create a new model for calculating operating leverage factor.

W

Weighted Average Cost of Capital (WACC) is a calculation of a firm's cost of capital where each category of capital is proportionately weighted. All sources of capital, including common stock, preferred stock, bonds, and any other long-term debt, are included in a WACC calculation that takes each source of funds and assigns a required rate of return to each individual source. A company's WACC increases as the beta and rate of return on equity increase because an increase in WACC denotes a decrease in valuation and an increase in risk. Baule (2019) suggested a method to estimate the cost of debt in a continuous-time framework with an infinite time horizon, and Qi and Xie (2016) identified some problems with the Weighted Average Cost of Capital (WACC) method.

Window Dressing is the process of compiling financial statements that give a more favorable view of an organization's performance that it is. One approach is to bring the record of invoices and deliveries into the current period's revenue instead of when they actually occurred. An interesting article by Bide (2018) adds to the technique of window dressing by explaining the methods used by department stores responded to the austerity and bomb damage of the Second World War by investing in display and visual merchandising to attract custom and rebuild their fashionable reputations. Taylor, Vithayathil, and Yim (2018) presented a more recent picture by broadening the act of window dressing by asking whether strategic engagement in social responsibility, rather than merely sponsoring environmental initiatives, contributes to increasing firm value.

Work-In-Process/Work-in-Progress (WIP) refers to partially finished goods awaiting completion. They include raw materials, labor, and overhead costs incurred for products that are at various stages of the production process. WIP is a component of the inventory account in the Balance Sheet. These costs are subsequently transferred to the finished goods account in the Balance Sheet and eventually to the Cost of Sales in the Income Statement. The terms Work-In-Progress and Work-In-Process are used interchangeably.

Working Capital Ratio calculates the amount of funding required for an organization's day to-day operations and identifies both liquidity and efficiency. Working capital is calculated by deducting current liabilities from current assets. The equation is:

Working capital = Current Assets minus Current Liabilities

A company must be alert to the amount of investment made in noncurrent assets, such as buildings and machinery. It needs to be even more alert to the money it is using in its daily operations. This is known as the investment in working capital. Insufficient working capital can cause a company to become bankrupt. The use of ratios assists a company to manage its working capital and also reveals to investors the immediate financial health of the company. A study by Khokhar (2019) compared the working capital investment of industrial firms and found that Canadian firms invest less in working capital than their U.S. counterparts.

Write-Down occur where companies have shown assets on their balance sheet that are over-valued. In this case, the assets may be written-down (i.e. reduced) in value to more conservatively reflect their value on a financial statement. The purpose of using estimated values such as provisions and write-downs of assets is to limit economic risk. Provisions should protect the entity against the adverse effects of future economic events that are possible to predict, and the write-downs of assets should protect the entity against overvaluation of its assets beyond their true value. However, in business practice, these estimates are often used by the boards of companies to manipulate financial results, both as a tool to increase as well as to decrease the result.

X

XBRL (eXtensible Business Reporting Language) is a software standard that was developed to improve the way in which financial data are communicated, making it easier to compile and share these data. Notably, eXtensible Business Reporting Language is an implementation of *XML* (Extensible Markup Language), which is a specification that is used for organizing and defining data online. XBRL uses tags to identify each piece of financial data, which then allows it to be used programmatically by an XBRL-compatible program. XBRL allows for easy transmission of data between businesses. In 2016, the SEC in the United States announced that it intended companies to structure financial statement data in their filings, including annual and quarterly reports, using the machine-readable XBRL format. The requirement was to be spread over several years with the greatest attention being given to the issues that confronted some companies doing the filing and less attention being paid to the users of the information.

Y

Yankee Bonds are issued in the U.S. domestic market by a borrower who is not a U.S. resident organization. There are several research articles on the subject, and Bruno and Hyun (2017) examined the reasons for many non-U.S. firms issuing bonds denominated in U.S. dollars.

Yield is the income from an investment expressed in various ways. Usually, the calculation is the return on an investment expressed as a percentage of its par value. A stock yield is calculated by dividing the annual dividend by the current market price of the stock. For example, a stock selling at $100 with an annual dividend of $10.00 per share has a yield of 10 percent (assuming a redemption price of $100). A yield cover is the curve on a graph on which the yield of fixed income securities is plotted against the duration period. A study by Lian, Ma, and Wang (2019) assessed how low interest rates affect investor behavior and concluded that individuals, understandably, are more likely to indulge in risk taking when interest rates are low.

Yield Curve is a curve drawn on a graph that shows the yield of fixed-income securities against the length of time there is until they mature. If the curve slopes upwards, it is an indication that investors can anticipate a premium for holding securities that have a substantial time to run. If there are possibilities of changes in the interest rate, the yield curve will change. A recent article by Secrest (2020) explored the meaning of yield curve inversion as well as the frequency with which it occurs within U.S. Treasury securities.

Z

Z-Score (Altman Z-score) is a numerical measurement that describes a value's relationship to the mean of a group of values. Z-score is measured in terms of standard deviations from the mean. If a Z-score is 0, it indicates that the data point's score is identical to the mean score. A Z-score of 1.0 would indicate a value that is one standard deviation from the mean. Z-scores may be positive or negative, with a positive value indicating the score is above the mean and a negative score indicating it is below the mean. In finance, Z-scores are measures of an observation's variability and can be used by traders to help determine market volatility. A recent article by Poudel, Prasad, and Jain (2020) focused on the relation between stock market returns and the probability of bankruptcy during an unexpected sudden shock.

Zero-Based Budgeting (ZBB) is a method of budgeting in which all expenses must be justified by managers for each financial period. The process of ZBB starts from a "zero base," and every function within an organization is analyzed for its needs and costs. Budgets are then built around what is needed for the upcoming period, regardless of whether each budget is higher or lower than the previous one. A study by Chinniah (2013) in the public sector argues that the method is helpful for all matching resource allocations with strategic goals. However, the method can be time-consuming and it can be difficult to quantify the returns on some expenditure, such as basic research.

Zero-Beta Portfolio is where investments are chosen so that the portfolio's value does not fluctuate as a result of market movements. The avoidance of systematic risk means that its return is the same as the risk-free rate. Thus, the return on a zero-beta portfolio is usually low without exposure to market volatility. However, such an approach does not enjoy the potential upswings in the value of the overall market. An article by Lee, Reeves, Tjahja, and Xie (2019) examines the need to assess overall market risk as an important part of investment management.

Zero Coupon Bond is a bond issued at a discount to mature at its face value. Usually, no interest is paid during the life of the bond and because such bonds offer the entire payment at maturity, they tend to fluctuate in price. This is a complex area attracting different types of research. One study directly relevant to the United States is by Caldeir and Torrent (2017).

Acronyms

AACSB	American Association of Collegiate Schools of Business
ABC	Activity-Based Costing
ACCA	Association of Chartered Certified Accountants
AI	Artificial Intelligence
AIA	Association of International Accountants
AICPA	American Institute of Certified Professional Accountants
APM	Alternative Performance Measures
APR	Annual Percentage Rate
ARR	Accounting Rate of Return
ASAF	Accounting Standards Advisory Forum
ASUs	Accounting Standards Updates
BDA	Big Data Analytics
CAPM	Capital Asset Pricing Model
CASB	Cost Accounting Standards Board
CIMA	Chartered Institute of Management Accountants
CVP	Cost–Volume-Profit
DCF	Discounted Cash Flow
DECC	Department of Energy and Climate Change
DJIA	Down Jones Industrial Average
EBITDA	Earnings Before Interest, Tax, Depreciation, and Amortization
EMH	Efficient Market Hypothesis
EOQ	Economic Order Quantity
EPS	Earnings Per Share
EVA	Economic Value Added
FASAC	Financial Accounting Standards Advisory Committee (U.S.)
FASB	Financial Accounting Standards Board (U.S.)
FIFO	First-In First-Out
FRC	Financial Reporting Council (UK)
GAAP	Generally Accepted Accounting Principle
GAAS	Generally Accepted Auditing Standards

GASB	Government Accounting Standards Board (U.S.)
GDP	Gross Domestic Product
HHI	Herfindahl-Hirschman Index
IAASB	International Auditing and Assurance Standards Board
IASB	International Accounting Standards Board
ICAEW	Institute of Chartered Accountants in England and Wales
IESBA	International Ethics Standards Board for Accountants
IFAC	International Federation of Accountants
IFRIC	International Financial Reporting Interpretations Committee
IFRS	International Financial Reporting Standards
IIRC	International Integrated Reporting Council
IPO	Initial Public Offering
KPI	Key Performance Indicators
NASDAQ	National Association of Securities Dealers Automated Quotation
NPV	Net Present Value
PEG	Price–Earnings-Growth Ratio
PER	Price/Earnings Ratio
PIEs	Public Interest Entities
ROCE	Return On Capital Employed
RPT	Related Party Transactions
SAR	Suspicious Activity Report
SASB	Sustainability Accounting Standards Boards
SEC	Securities and Exchange Commission (U.S.)
SEDAR	System for Electronic Document Analysis and Retrieval
SIC	Standards Interpretation Committee (International)
SOX	Sarbanes-Oxley Act
TQM	Total Quality Management
WACC	Weighted Average Cost of Capital
WIP	Work In Progress
XBRL	eXtensible Business Reporting Language
ZBB	Zero-Based Budgeting

References

Abdel-Khalik, A.R. 2019. "Failing Faithful Representations of Financial Statements: Issues in Reporting Financial Instruments." *ABACUS* 55, no. 4, 676–708. doi:10.1111/abac.12176

Abel, I., and K. Lehmann. 2019. "Real and Monetary Theories of the Interest Rate." *International Journal of Political Economy* 48, no. 4, 353–63. doi:10.1080/08911916.2019.1693159

Abouee-Mehrizi, H., O. Baron, O. Berman, and D. Chen. September 2019. "Managing Perishable Inventory Systems with Multiple Priority Classes." *Production and Operations Management* 28, no. 9, 2305–22. doi:10.1111/poms.13058

Abugri, B.A., and T. T. Osah. 2021. "Derivative Use, Ownership Structure and Lending Activities of US Banks." *Journal of Economics & Finance* 45, no. 1, 146–70. doi:10.1007/s12197-020-09535-3

Adhikari, S., B. Guragai, and A. Seetharaman. 2020. "Market Response to Audited Internal Control Weakness Disclosures." *Journal of Forensic Accounting Research* 5, no. 1, 2–20. doi:10.2308/JFAR-19-016

Afonso, A., F. Huart, J. Jalles, and P. Stanek. February 2019. "Assessing the Sustainability of External Imbalances in the European Union." *World Economy* 42, no. 2, 320–48. doi:10.1111/twec.12709

Almeida, H. 2019. "Is It Time to Get Rid of Earnings-per-Share (EPS)?" *Review of Corporate Finance Studies* 8, no. 1, 174–206. doi:10.1093/rcfs/cfy010

Altman, E.I. 1968. "Financial Ratios, Discriminant Analysis and the Prediction of Corporate Bankruptcy." *The Journal of Finance* 23, no. 4, pp. 589–609.

El-Ammar, C. May 2020. *"iBalanced Scorecard: An Effective Strategy Implementation in Lebanese Government Authorities." Review of International Comparative Management/ Revista de Management Comparat International* 21, Issue. 2, 146–64. doi:10.24818/RMCI.2020.2.146

Ammar, S., A. Annabi, T. Sim, and R. Wright. 2020. "Measuring Corporate Dividend Risk by Using a Monte Carlo Simulation Model." *Journal of Accounting & Finance* 20, no. 4, 135–49. doi:10.33423/jaf.v20i4.3124

Apriwandi, Y.M. Pratiwi. 2019. "The Influence of Social Pressure, Responsibility and Procedural Fairness Towards the Creation of Budgetary Slack: An Experimental Research." *Global Business and Management Research: An International Journal* 11, pp. 9–21.

Ardern, D., and M. Aiken. June 2005. "An Accounting History of Capital Maintenance: Legal Precedents for Managerial Autonomy in the United Kingdom." *Accounting Historians Journal* 32, no. 1, pp. 23–60.

Arnold, A., R. Ellis, and V. Krishnan. Fall 2018. "Toward Effective Use of the Statement of Cash Flows." *Journal of Business & Behavioral Sciences* 30, no. 2, pp. 46–62.

Ashton, J.K., and A. Gregoriou. 2017. "Does an Overdraft Facility Influence the Customer Costs of Using a Personal Current Account?" *International Journal of the Economics of Business* 24, no. 1, 1–26. doi:10.1080/13571516.2016.1 222990

Ataullah, A., A. Higson, and M. Tippett. 2007. "The Distributional Properties of the Debt to Equity Ratio: Some Implications for Empirical Research." *ABACUS* 43, no. 2, 111–35. doi:10.1111/j.1467-6281.2007.00222.x

Autre, R., F. Bova, and D. Soberman. April 2015. "When Gray Is Good: Gray Markets and Market-Creating Investments." *Production and Operations Management Society* 24, no. 4, 547–59. doi:10.1111/poms.12254

Ayres, D., J. Campbell, J. Chyz, and J. Shipman. 2019. "Do Financial Analysts Compel Firms to Make Accounting Decisions? Evidence from Goodwill Impairments." *Review of Accounting Studies* 24, 1214–51. doi:10.1007/s11142-019-09512-0

Babaei, Z., and F. Shahveisi. 2017. "Studying the Information Content, Economic Value Added, Liquidity, and Activity in Market Value Added Determination." *International Journal of Economic Perspectives* 11, no. 1, pp. 843–850.

Baciu, R., and P. Brezeanu. 2018. "Sector Analysis – Maintenance and Repair of Motor Vehicles and Retail Trade of Motor Vehicle Parts and Accessories." *Finance: Challenges of the Future* 18, no. 20, 97–107.

Bai, X., J. Chang, and J. Li. 2019. "How Do International Joint Ventures Build Legitimacy Effectively in Emerging Economies? CSR, Political Ties, or Both?" *Management International Review* 59, 387–412. doi:10.1007/s11575-019-00382-x

Baker, C.R. December 2017. "The Influence of Accounting Theory on the FASB Conceptual Framework." *Accounting Historians Journal* 44, no. 2, 109–24. doi:10.2308/aahj-10555

Banko, J.C., and L. Zhou. Summer 2010. "Callable Bonds Revisited." *Financial Management* 39, 613–41.

Baranes, A.I. September 2020. "Intangible Assets and the Financialized Business Enterprise: A Veblen-Commons Approach." *Journal of Economic Issues* 54, no. 3, 692–709. doi:10.1080/00213624.2020.1778973

Barker, R., and A. Teixeira. 2014. "Gaps in the IFRS Conceptual Framework." *Accounting in Europe* 15, no. 2, 153–66. doi:10.1080/17449480.2018.147 6771

Barnes, P. August 1996. "The Regulation of Insider Dealing in the UK: Some Empirical Evidence Concerning Share Prices, Merger Bids and Bidders' Advising Merchant Bank." *Applied Financial Economics* 6, no. 4, pp. 383–391.

Batistic, S., and P. van der Laken. 2019. "History, Evolution and Future of Big Data and Analytics: A Bibliometric Analysis of Its Relationship to Performance in Organizations." *British Journal of Management* 30, 229–51. doi:10.1111/1467-8551.12340

Batten, J., K. Khaw, and M. Young. 2014. "Convertible Bond Pricing Models." *Journal of Economic Surveys* 28, no. 5, 775–803.

Baule, R. 2019. "The Cost of Debt Capital Revisited." *Business Research* 12, 721–53. doi:10.1007/s40685-018-0070-6

Baumers, M., L. Beltrametti, A. Gasparre, and R. Hague. 2017. "Informing Additive Manufacturing Technology Adoption: Total Cost and the Impact of Capacity Utilization." *International Journal of Production Research* 55, no. 23, 6957–70. doi:10.1080/00207543.2017.1334978

Bayar, O., T. Chemmanur, and X. Tian. September 2020. "Peer Monitoring, Syndication, and the Dynamics of Venture Capital Interactions: Theory and Evidence." *Journal of Financial and Quantitative Analysis* 55, no. 6, 1875–914. doi:10.1017/S0022109019000218

Bazdan, Z. 2010. "Sell When the Violins Are Playing – Buy When the Cannons Rumble. Case Study: Technical Analysis and Chartists." *Naše gospodarstvo*, 3–4, 11-18.

Bebchuk, L.A., A. Brav, and W. Jiang. June 2015. "The Long-Term Effects of Hedge Fund Activism." *Columbia Law Review* 115, no. 5, pp. 1085–1155.

Benos, Evangelos, Richard Payne, and Michalis Vasios. February 2020. "Centralized Trading, Transparency, and Interest Rate Swap Market Liquidity: Evidence from the Implementation of the Dodd–Frank Act." *Journal of Financial & Quantitative Analysis* 55, no. 1, 159–92. doi:10.1017/S0022109018001527

Berglund, N., D.R. Herrmann, and B.P. Lawson. 2018. "Managerial Ability and the Accuracy of the Going Concern Opinion." *Accounting and the Public Interest* 18, no. 1, 29–52. doi:10.2308/apin-52125

Berland, N., and T. Boyns. 2002. "The Development of Budgetary Control in France and Britain from the 1920s to the 1960s: A Comparison." *The European Accounting Review* 11, no. 2, pp. 329–356.

Betancourt, L., and J.H. Irving. November 2019. "The Challenge of Accounting for Goodwill Impact of a Possible Return to Amortization." *CPA Journal*, pp. 46–51.

Bhuller, M., M. Mogstad, and K.G. Salvanes. October 2017. "Life-Cycle Earnings, Education Premiums, and Internal Rates of Return." *Journal of Labor Economics* 35, no. 4, 993–1030. doi:10.1086/692509

Biddle, G.C., G.S. Seow, and A.F. Siegel. Fall 1995. "Relative versus Incremental Information Content." *Contemporary Accounting Research* 12, no. 1, 1–23. doi:10.1111/j.1911-3846.1995.tb00478.x

Bide, B. 2018. "More Than Window Dressing: Visual Merchandising and Austerity in London's West End, 1945–50." *Business History* 60, no. 7, 983–1003. doi:10.1080/00076791.2017.1400531

Bilici, H., and I. Dalci. 2008. "Gearing Multiple Cost Drivers of Activity-Based Costing into Operating Leverage Model for Better Production and Profit Planning Decisions." *Journal of Business & Management* 14, no. 1, pp. 61–75.

Black, M. January/February 2020. "Are Incentive Stock Options Worth the Trouble?" *The Corporate Governance Advisor* 8, pp. 8–10.

Blaywais, R., and M. Rosenboim. December 2019. "The Effect of Cognitive Load on Economic Decisions." *Managerial & Decision Economics* 40, no. 8, 993–99. doi:10.1002/mde.3085

Bleibtreu, C., and U. Stefani. January 2018. "The Effects of Mandatory Audit Firm Rotation on Client Importance and Audit Industry Concentration." *The Accounting Review* 93, no. 1, 1–27. doi:10.2308/accr-51728

Bok, B., S. Choi, and D. Farber. July 2020. "Managerial Ability and Income Smoothing." *The Accounting Review* 95, no. 4, 1–22. doi:10.2308/accr-52600

Bouri, E., M. Das, R. Gupta, and D. Roubaudd. 2018. "Spillovers between Bitcoin and Other Assets During Bear and Bull Markets." *Applied Economics* 50, no. 55, 5935–49. doi:10.1080/00036846.2018.1488075

Bowden, R.J., and P.N. Posch. December 2011. "The Bonus Pool, Mark to Market and Free Cash Flow: Producer Surplus and Its Vesting in the Financial Markets." *Applied Financial Economics* 21, no. 24, 1843–57. doi:10.1080/09603107.2011.595679

Boyns, T., and J.R. Edwards. July 1997. "The Construction of the Cost Accounting System in Britain to 1900: The Case of Coal Iron and Steel Industries 0097." *Business History* 39, no. 3, 1–29. doi:10.1080/00076799700000097

Boyns, T., J.R. Edwards, and M. Nikitin. September 2010. "The Development of Industrial Accounting in Britain and France Before 1880: A Comparative Study of Accounting Literature and Practice." *European Accounting Review* 6, no. 3, 393–437. doi:10.1080/096381897336656

Braam, G., and R. Peeters. 2018. "Corporate Sustainability Performance and Assurance on Sustainability Reports: Diffusion of Accounting Practices in the Realm of Sustainable Development." *Corporate Social Responsibility and Environmental Management* 25, pp. 164–181.

Bradshaw, K. 2019. "Stakeholder Collaboration as an Alternative to Cost-Benefit Analysis." *Brigham Young University Law Review*, pp. 657–721.

Brent, R. 2019. "A Cost–Benefit Analysis of Hearing Aids, Including the Benefits of Reducing the Symptoms of Dementia." *Applied Economics* 51, no. 28, 3091–103. doi:10.1080/00036846.2018.1564123

Brezina, I., J. Pekár, Z. Cicková, and M. Reiff. 2016. "Herfindahl–Hirschman Index Level of Concentration Values Modification and Analysis of Their Change." *Central European Journal of Operations Research* 24, 49–72. doi:10.1007/s10100-014-0350-y

Brogan, J. February 2016. "What's the Deal with Algorithms? Your 101 Guide to the Computer Codes That Are Shaping the Ways We Live." *Future Tense* 10, no. 29, 1–4.

Bromwell, T. August 2017. "What Is the Public Interest Role of Accountants?" *The CPA Journal* 87, no. 8, 6–7.

Bronson, C., and D. Smith. 2017. "Swindled or Served? A Survey of Payday Lending Customers in Southeast Alabama." *The Southern Business and Economic Journal* 40, no. 1, 16–32.

Bruno, V., and H.S. Shin. March 2017. "Global Dollar Credit and Carry Trades: 2017 A Firm-Level Analysis." *Review of Financial Studies* 30, no. 3, 703–49. doi:10.1093/rfs/hhw099

Bui, D.Y., D. Chance, and C. Stephens. 2019. "Does the Choice Between Listing on the NYSE Versus Nasdaq Matter? An Examination of Firms that Voluntarily Move from the NYSE to Nasdaq." *Journal of Accounting & Finance (2158–3625)* 19, no. 7, 18–48. doi:10.33423/jaf.v19i7.2560

Button, R., S. Knott, C. MacManus, and M. Willison. 2015. "Desperate Adventurers and Men of Straw: The Failure of City of Glasgow Bank and Its Enduring Impact on the UK Banking System." *Bank of England Quarterly Bulletin* Q1, pp. 23–35.

Byron, P. February 2020. "What Is Artificial Intelligence?" *Journal of Accountancy* 229, no. 2, 1–4. https://www.journalofaccountancy.com/issues/2020/feb/what-is-artificial-intelligence.html

Caldeira, J., and H. Torrent. January 2017. "Forecasting the US Term Structure of Interest Rates Using Nonparametric Functional Data Analysis." *Journal of Forecasting* 36, no. 1, 56–73. doi:10.1002/for.2414

Cameron, R., J. Lewis, and L. Pfeiffer. 2014. "The FIFO Experience: A Gladstone Case Study." *Australian Bulletin of Labour* 40, no. 2, 221–241.

Camfferman, K., and S.A. Zeff. 2015. *Aiming for Global Accounting Standards: The International Accounting Standards Board, 2001–2011,* 661. Oxford: Oxford University Press.

Capelle-Blancard, G., and A. Petit. June 2019. "Every Little Helps? ESG News and Stock Market Reaction." *Journal of Business Ethics* 157, no. 2, 543–65. doi:10.1007/s10551-017-3667-3

Caporalea, G., and A. Plastun. 2019. "On Stock Price Overreactions: Frequency, Seasonality and Information Content." *Journal of Applied Economics* 22, no. 1, 602–21. doi:10.1080/15140326.2019.1692509

Cappelli, P., M. Conyon, and D. Almeda. January 2020. "Social Exchange and the Effects of Employee Stock Options." *HR Review* 73, no. 1, 124–52. doi:10.1177/0019793919827934

Căpușneanu, S., and D.M. Martinescu. 2010. "Convergence of ABC and ABM Principles – Guarantee of a Performant Management." *Theoretical and Applied Economics* 17, no. 10, pp. 93–102.

Carey, T., and R.A. Dyson. April 2017. "Implementing ASU 2016–14 on the Presentation of Not-for-Profit Financial Statements." *The CPA Journal*, 24–32.

Catuogno, S., S. Saggese, F. Sarto, and R. Vigano. 2016. "Shedding Light on the Aim of Stock Options: A Literature Review." *Journal of Management Governance* 20, 387–411. doi:10.1007/s10997-015-9318-0

Chaklader, B., and P. Aggarwal. December 2011. "Declaration of Bonus Debenture: A Case of Britannia Industries Limited." *Journal of Case Research* 2, no. 2, pp. 93–107.

Chander, S., and M. Vishakha. October 2010. "Disclosure of Intangible Assets in Indian Drugs and Pharmaceutical Industry." IUP *Journal of Accounting Research & Audit Practices* 9, no. 4, pp. 7–23.

Chang, W.J., S.J. Monahan, A. Ouazad, and F.P. Vasvari. January 2021. "The Higher Moments of Future Earnings." *Accounting Review* 96, no 1, 91–116. doi:10.2308/TAR-2015-0413

Chapman, K., and J.R Green. January 2018. "Analysts' Influence on Managers' Guidance." *The Accounting Review.* 93, no. 1, 45–69. doi:10.2308/accr-51778

Chen, M., Q. Wu, and B. Yang. 2019. "How Valuable Is FinTech Innovation?" *The Review of Financial Studies* 32, no. 5, 2062–2106.

Chen, Y., A. Ho, and L. Wang. Spring 2016. "Does Earnings Management Explain the Long-Term Performance of Capital Reduction Firms?" *International Review of Accounting, Banking and Finance.* 8, no. 1, 54–78.

Chetan, D. January 2011. "Are Investment Expectations Rational, Adaptive Or Regressive?" *Economic Inquiry* 49, no. 1, 212–225. doi:10.1111/j.1465-7295.2010.00305

Chiek, A.N., and M.N. Akpan. March 2016. "Determinants of Stock Prices During Dividend Announcements: An Evaluation of Firms' Variable Effects in Nigeria's Oil and Gas Sector." *OPEC Energy Review* 40, no. 1, 69–90. doi:10.1111/opec.12063

Chilakapati, C., and D. Rochford. June/July 2020. "Understanding and Assessing Machine Learning Algorithms." *CFO publishing* 36, no. 3, 16–17.

Chinniah, A. 2013. "An Effective Role of an Accounting in Human Resource Management to Increase an Organizational Management and Decision-Making." *CLEAR International Journal of Research in Commerce & Management* 3, no. 5, pp. 1–17.

Choi, Y., and S. Young. 2015. "Transitory Earnings Components and the Two Faces of Non-Generally Accepted Accounting Principles Earnings." *Accounting and Finance* 55, pp. 75–103.

Choi, Y., S.J. Jordan, and S. Ok. 2012. "Dividend-Rollover Effect and the Ad Hoc Black-Scholes Model." *Journal of Futures Markets* 32, no. 8, 742–772. doi: 10.1002/fut

Chong, V.C., and D. Sudarso. 2016. "The Effect of Organizational Ethical Climate and Peer Monitoring Control Systems on Budgetary Slack: An Experimental Study." *Asia-Pacific Management Accounting Journal*, 11, no. 2, pp. 41–63.

Chow, R.A., and J. Zorthian. 2010. "NFTs and the Cryptic Art Revolution." *Time Magazine* 197, nos. 11–12, pp. 36–43.

Chung. H., C.H. Sonu, Y. Zang, and J. Choi. 2019. "Opinion Shopping to Avoid a Going Concern Audit Opinion and Subsequent Audit Quality." *Auditing: A Journal of Practice & Theory American Accounting Association* 38, no. 2, 101–123. doi:10.2308/ajpt-52154

Claye, R. November 2000. "A Tall Order." *Director* 54, no. 4, p. 92.

Clout, V., J.R. Willett, and T. Smith. 2016. "Analysing the Market–Book Value Relation in Large Australian and US firms: Implications for Fundamental Analysis and the Market–Book Ratio." *Accounting and Finance* 56, 1017–1040.

Cohney, S., D. Hofman, D. Sklarof, J. Wishnick, and D. Hoffman. 2020. "Coin-Operated Capitalism." *Columbia Law Review* 119, no. 3, pp. 591–676.

Collins, J.C. 2017. "Microsoft Excel: 3 Ways to Calculate Internal Rate of Return in Excel." *Journal of Accountancy* 223, no. 2, pp. 25–26.

Concepts and Standards Research Study Committee. 1964. "The Business Entity Concept." *Accounting Review*.

Cong, Y., H. Du, and M.A. Vasarhelyi. Fall 2018. "Are XBRL Files Being Accessed?" *Evidence from the SEC EDGAR Log File Dataset Journal of Information Systems American Accounting Association* 32, no. 3, 23–29. doi:10.2308/isys-51885

Cooper, R., and R. Slagmulder. 1999. "Develop Profitable New Products with Target Costing." *Sloan Management Review* 40, no. 4, p. 333.

Corbett, C. September 2018. "How Sustainable is Big Data." *Production and Operations Management* 27, no. 9, 1685–1695. doi:10.1111/poms.12837 ISSN 1059-1478|EISSN 1937-5956|18|2709|1685

Couts, A. Andrew (December 12, 2013). "Wow. Dogecoin is the most Internet thing to happen, ever". *Digital Trends*. Archived *from the original on December 14, 2013*. Retrieved December 12, 2013.

Crittenden, E. 2017. "Advisers Show a Return to Cash, Continue to Favor ETFs." *Journal of Financial Planning* 30, no. 6, p. 18.

Curtis. A., M.F. Lewis-Western, and S. Toynbee. September 05, 2015. "Historical Cost Measurement and the Use of DuPont Analysis by Market Participants." *Review of Accounting Studies* 20, no. 3, 1210–1245. doi:10.1007/s11142-015-9334-y

Dahlgaard., J.J., L. Reyes, C.K. Chen, and S.M. Dahlgaard-Park. 2019. "Evolution and Future of Total Quality Management: Management Control and Organisational Learning." *Total Quality Management & Business Excellence* 2019, no. 30, S1–S16. doi:10.1080/14783363.2019.1 665776

Das. S., C.M. Kuhnen, and S. Nagel. January 2020. "Socioeconomic Status and Macroeconomic Expectations." *Review of Financial Studies* 33, no. 1, 395–432. doi:10.1093/rfs/hhz041

De Vries, C.E. September 2017. "*Benchmarking Brexit: How the British Decision to Leave Shapes EU Public Opinion.*" *Journal of Common Market Studies*, Supplement 1, no. 55, 38–53. doi:10.1111/jcms.12579

Del Mundo, C. 2019. "How Countries Seek to Strengthen Anti-Money Laundering Laws in Response to the Panama Papers, and the Ethical Implications of Incentivizing Whistleblowers." *Northwestern Journal of International Law & Business* 40, no. 1, pp. 87–122.

Dennis, I. 2018. "What is a Conceptual Framework for Financial Reporting?" *Accounting in Europe* 15, no. 3, 374–401. doi:10.1080/17449480.2018.14 96269

Dohrer, B., L. Delahanty, and A. Goldman. August 01, 2020. "What to Consider Before Deferring ASB Reporting Standards the Effective Date Delay was Granted to Provide Relief During the Coronavirus Pandemic." *Journal of Accountancy*.

Donahue, S., J. Letalien, and B. Soares. November 2020. "Going Public through a SPAC: Legal Considerations for SPAC Sponsors and Private Companies." *Insights* 34, no 11, pp. 28–33.

Dong., M., and X.J. Zhang. 2018. "Selective Trading of Available-for-Sale Securities: Evidence from U.S. Commercial Banks." *European Accounting Review* 27, no. 3, 467–493, doi:10.1080/09638180.2017.1304227

Dou., Y., R.W. Masulis, and Z.J. Ronald. December 2019. "Shareholder Wealth Consequences of Insider Pledging of Company Stock as Collateral for Personal Loans." *Review of Financial Studies* 32, no. 12, 4810–4854. doi:10.1093/rfs/hhz034

Du, Y., S. Xue, and L.Y. Liu. January 2019. "Robust Upper Bounds for American Put Options." *Journal of Futures Markets* 39, no. 1, 3–14. doi:10.1002/fut.21961

Du, B. October 2017. "How Useful Is Basel III's Liquidity Coverage Ratio? Evidence From US Bank Holding." *Companies European Financial Management* 23, no. 5, 902–919. doi:10.1111/eufm.12116

Dugdale, D., and C.J. Jones. 1997. "How Many Companies Use ABC for Stock Valuation? A Comment on Innes and Mitchell's Questionnaire Findings." *Management Accounting Research* 8, 233–240.

Dulk, M. 2016. "The Sign of Cash Flows: A Source of Error in Present Value Approximations." *The Engineering Economist* 61, no. 2, 79–94 doi:10.1080/0013791X22016.1149262

Easton., D.P., and S.J. Monahan. 2016. "Review of Recent Research on Improving Earnings Forecasts and Evaluating Accounting-based Estimates of the Expected Rate of Return on Equity Capital." *ABACUS* 52, no. 1, 35–58. doi:10.1111/abac.12064

Edmans, A., V.W. Fang, and K.A. Lewellen. 2017. "Equity Vesting and Investment." *The Society for Financial Studies* 30, no. 7, pp. 2229–2271.

Edwards, J.R. 2014. "Different from What Has Hitherto Appeared on this Subject': John Clark, Writing Master and Accomptant 1738." *ABACUS* 50, no. 2, 227–244. doi:10.1111/j.1467-6281.2012.00375.x

Elam, D. 2020. "Convergence Not: A Socionomic Analysis of a Globalization Failure." *Journal of Applied Financial Research* 1, pp. 19–26.

Elkington, J. 1997. *Cannibals with Forks: The Triple Bottom Line of 21st Century Business.* Oxford, UK: Capstone Publishing.

Ernst, P. 2017. "On the Arbitrage Price of European Call Options." *Stochastic Models* 33, no. 1, pp. 48–58.

Ertan, A., S. Lewellen, and J.K. Thomas. Fall 2020. "Do Profit Margins Expand for High Growth Firms?" *Journal of Management Accounting Research. American Accounting Association* 32, no. 3, 117–135. doi:10.2308/jmar-18-079

Farghera, N., B. Sidhub, A. Tarcac, and W. Zyl. 2019. "Accounting for Financial Instruments with Characteristics of Debt and Equity: Finding a Way Forward." *Accounting & Finance* 59, 7–58. doi:10.1111/acfi.12280

Farm, A. 2020. "Pricing in Practice in Consumer Markets." *Journal of Post Keynesian Economics* 43, no. 1, 61–75. doi:10.1080/01603477.2019.1616562

Financial Accounting Standards Board. 2018. Proposed Taxonomy Improvements for Proposed Accounting Standards Update—Debt (Topic 470) Simplifying the Classification of Debt in a Classified Balance Sheet (Current versus Noncurrent) Issued: October 12.

Fisher., T.C., I. Gavious, and J. Martel. 2019. "Earnings Management in Chapter 11 Bankruptcy." *ABACUS* 55, no. 2. doi:10.1111/abac.12158

Fleckenstein, M., F.A. Longstaff, and H. Lustig. 2017. "Deflation Risk." *The Review of Financial Studies* 30, no. 8, pp. 2720–2758.

Foley, S., J.R. Karlsen, and T.J. Putninis. 2019. "Sex, Drugs, and Bitcoin: How Much Illegal Activity Is Financed through Cryptocurrencies?" Downloaded from https://academic.oup.com/rfs/article-abstract/32/5/1798/5427781

Fabozzi, F.J., R.J. Shiller, and R.S. Tunaru. Fall 2020. "A 30-Year Perspective on Property Derivatives: What Can Be Done to Tame Property Price Risk?" *Journal of Economic Perspectives* 34, no. 4, pp. 121–145.

Franz, D.R. May 2018. *"Back to the Future (Or How a Product Last Sold Almost 60 Years Ago Resulted in a Current Financial Statement Restatement)."* Issues in Accounting Education 33, no. 2, 9–17. doi:10.2308/iace-51968

Frestad, D. 2018. "Managing Earnings Risk Under SFAS 133/IAS 39: The Case of Cash Flow Hedges." *Rev Quant Finan Acc* 51, pp. 159–197. doi:10.1007/s11156-017-0667-4

Fuh, U.H., and S.F. Luo. 2018. "Buy-and-Hold Mean-Variance Portfolios with a Random Exit Strategy." *Quantitative Finance* 18, no. 8, 1365–1377. doi:10.1080/14697688.2017.1372619

Galbraith, K. 2009. *The Great Crash 1929*, Reprint Edition. Mariner Books.

Gao, P., and G. Zhang. November 2019. "Auditing Standards, Professional Judgment, and Audit Quality." *The Accounting Review American Accounting Association* 94, no. 6, 201–225. doi: 0.2308/accr-52389

Gara, A., E. Haverstock, and S. Klebnikov. December 2020. "The Looming SPAC Meltdown." *SPAC Meltdown, Forbes* 203, no. 6, pp. 114–119.

Garcia, R.J., and D. von Winterfeldt. 2016. "Defender–Attacker Decision Tree Analysis to Combat Terrorism." *Risk Analysis* 36, no. 12, 2258–2271. doi:10.1111/risa.12574

Gaspars-Wieloch, H.C. 2019. "Net Present Value Estimation Under Uncertainty." *Central European Journal of Operations Research*, 179–197. doi:10.1007/s10100-017-0500

Gillan, S.L. 2006. "Recent Developments in Corporate Governance: An Overview." *Journal of Corporate Finance* 12, pp. 381–402.

Gold, S. 2018. "Stock Market Algorithmic Trading: A Test of Bollinger Bands Incorporating the Squeeze Effect and MACD Conditions." *Journal of Applied Financial Research* 1, 13–28.

Gómez Martínez, R., M. Prado Román, and P. Plaza Casado. 2019. "Big Data Algorithmic Trading Systems Based on Investors' Mood." *Journal of Behavioral Finance* 20, no. 2, 227–238. doi:10.1080/15427560.2018.1506786

Gornik-Tomaszewski, S., and Y.C. Choi. 2018. "The Conceptual Framework: Past, Present, and Future." *Review of Business: Interdisciplinary Journal on Risk and Society* 38, no. 1, pp. 47–58.

Gray, P. Spring 2006. "Little Is New Under The Sun But…" *Information Systems Management*, pp. 89–93.

Güleç, O., and A. Arda. 2019. "Investigation of Cash Flow Profiles: Evidence From Turkey." *Journal of Accounting & Finance*, 555–568. doi:10.25095/ mufad.607209

Haber, J., and C. Schryver. April 2017. "How to Create Key Performance Indicators." *The CPA Journal.* 24–30. New York State Society of Certified Public Accountants.

Halsey, J.C., and B.J. Halsey. May 2020. "Bitcoin's IRS, SEC, and CFTC Treatment: The Current State of Affairs." *Journal of Financial Service Professionals* 74, no. 3, 50–55.

Hansen, E.G., and S. Schaltegger. 2018. "Sustainability Balanced Scorecards and their Architectures: Irrelevant or Misunderstood?" *Journal of Business Ethics* 150, 937–952. doi:10.1007/s10551-017-3531-5

Hardies, K., D. Breesch, and J.L. Branson. 2016. "Do (Fe)Male Auditors Impair Audit Quality? Evidence from Going-Concern Opinions." *European Accounting Review* 25, no. 1, 7–34, doi:10.1080/09638180.2014.921445

Harikumar, T., and M.E. De Boyrie. 2004. "Evaluation of Black-Scholes and GARCH Models Using Currency Call Options Data." *Review of Quantitative Finance and Accounting*, 23, no. 4, pp. 299–312.

Haron, R., and N. Nomran. 2016. "Determinants of Working Capital Management Before, During, and After the Global Financial Crisis of 2008: Evidence From Malaysia." *The Journal of Developing Areas* 50, no. 5, 461–468.

Heller. P. 2004. "Are Governments Overextended? Assessing the Spectrum of a Government's Debts and Its Exposure to Risk." *World Economics* 5, no. 4, 1–31.

Herath, H., and X. Lu. 2018. "Inference of Economic Truth from Financial Statements for Detecting Earnings Management: Inventory Costing Methods from an Information Economics Perspective." https://onlinelibrary.wiley. com/doi/abs/10.1002/mde.2912

Herdyanto, R., and H. Yudawisastra. 2019. "The Financial Distress Indication on Mining Industry of Oil and Gas Sub-Sectors in Indonesia." *Global Business & Management Research* 11, no. 1, pp. 302–306.

Herron, T.L., and C.P.A. Herbold. March 2019. "Private company GAAP alternatives: It's Not too Late." *Journal of Accountancy*, pp. 1–8.

Hess, D. 2007. "Social Reporting and New Governance Regulation: The Prospects of Achieving Corporate Accountability Through Transparency." *Business Ethics Quarterly* 17, no. 3, 453–476. ISSN 1052-150X

Hiemann, M. November 2020. "Earnings and Firm Value in the Presence of Real Options." *Accounting Review* 95, no. 6, 263–289. doi:10.2308/tar-2017-0019

Higgins, C., and A. Huque. 2015. "Public Money and Mickey Mouse Evaluating Performance and Accountability in the Hong Kong Disneyland Joint Venture Public–Private Partnership." *Public Management Review* 17, no. 8, 1103–1123, doi:10.1080/14719037.2014.881533

Hirsch, Y. 1986. *Stock Trader's Almanac*. New York, NY: Reed Business Information.

Hirsch, Y. 2016. *Stock Trader's Almanac*. New York, NY: Reed Business Information.

Hirsch, Y. October 2016. *ILR Review* 69, no. 5, 1191–1215. doi:10.1177/0019793915625214

Ho, K., S. Lee., C. Lin, and M. Yu. 2017. "A Comparative Analysis of Accounting-Based Valuation Models." *Journal of Accounting, Auditing & Finance* 32, no. 4, 561–575, doi:10.1177/0148558X15623043

Ho., C.Y., and D. Li. May 2014. "A Mirror of History: China's Bond Market. 1921-42." *Economic History Review* 67, no. 2, 409–434. doi:10.1111/1468-0289.12026

Hoang, K., S.E. Salterio, and J. Sylph. 2018. "Barriers to Transferring Auditing Research to Standard Setters." *Accounting Perspectives* 17, no. 3, 427–452 © CAAA/ACPC doi:10.1111/1911-3838.12181

Hoang., T.H.V., W. Przychodzen, J. Przychodzen., and E.A. Segbotangni. March 2020. "Does it Pay to be Green? A Disaggregated Analysis of U.S. Firms with Green Patents." *Business Strategy & the Environment* 29, no. 3, 1331–1361. doi:10.1002/bse.2437

Holderness, C. Winter 2019. "The Effect of Shareholder Approval of Equity Issuances Around the World." *Journal of Applied Corporate Finance* 31, no. 1, pp. 23–41.

Holub, M., and J. Johnson. 2018. "Bitcoin Research Across Disciplines." *The Information Society* 34, no. 2, 114–126. doi:10.1080/01972243.2017. 1414094

Hong, K., K. Park, and J. Yu. 2018. "Crowding Out in a Dual Currency Regime? Digital Versus Fiat Currency." *Emerging Markets Finance & Trade* 54, no. 11, 2495–2515. Online doi:https://doi.org/10.1080/1540496X.2018.1452732

Hope, O., and H. Lu. July 04, 2020. "Economic Consequences of Corporate Governance Disclosure: Evidence from the 2006 SEC Regulation on Related-Party Transactions." *The Accounting Review* 95, no. 4, 263–29. doi: 10.2308/accr-52608

Abouee-Mehrizi, H., O. Baron, O. Berman, and D. Chen. 2019. "Managing Perishable Inventory Systems with Multiple Priority Classes." *Production & Operations Management* 28, no. 9, 2305–2322. doi:10.1111/poms.13058

Huselid, M.A. 2018. "The Science and Practice of Workforce Analytics: Introduction to the HRM Special Issue." *Human Resource Management* 57, 679–684. doi:10.1002/hrm.21916

Hussain, N., U. Rigoni, and R.P. Orij. 2018. "Corporate Governance and Sustainability Performance: Analysis of Triple Bottom Line Performance." *J Bus Ethics* 149, 411–432. doi:10.1007/s10551-016-3099-5

Hussey, R., and A. Ong. 2018. "Pick a Number: Internationalizing U.S." *Accounting*, 2nd ed. Business Expert Press.

Hussey, R., and A. Ong. 2020. *A Non-Technical Guide to International Accounting*. Business Expert Press.

Hussey, R., and A. Ong. 2021. *Accounting for Business*. Business Expert Press.

Hussey, R., and A. Ong. 2018. *Strategic Cost Analysis*. Business Expert Press.

Ikeziri, L.M., F.B.D. Souza, and M.C. Guptab. 2019. "Theory of Constraints: Review and Bibliometric Analysis." *International Journal of Production Research* 57, no. 15–16, 5068–5102. doi:10.1080/00207543.2018.1518602

Ilter, C. 2018. "Cheque kiting? I Have An Idea." *Journal of Financial Crime* 25, no. 2, 589–597. doi:10.1108/JFC-05-2017-0036

Isil, O., and M.T. Hernke. 2017. "The Triple Bottom Line: A Critical Review from a Transdisciplinary Perspective Business Strategy and the Environment Bus." *Business Strategy and the Environment* 26, 1235–1251. Published online 30 October 2017 in Wiley Online Library doi:10.1002/bse.1982

Lia, J.F., and Z.X. Lin. 2016. "Social Benefit Expenditures and Stagflation: Evidence from the United States." *Applied Economics* 48, no. 55, 5340–5347 doi:10.1080/00036846.2016.1176118

Jaggia, S., and S. Thosar. July 2019. "An Evaluation of Chapter 11 Bankruptcy Filings in a Competing Risks Framework." *Journal of Economics & Finance* 43, no. 3, 569–581. doi:10.1007/s12197-018-9458-6

Jarrow, R., and P. Protter. January 2013. "Positive Alphas, Abnormal Performance, and Illusory Arbitrage." *Mathematical Finance* 23, no. 1, pp. 39–56.

Jiang, X., and Q. Kang. July 2020. "Cross-Sectional PEG ratios, Market Equity Premium, and Macroeconomic Activity." *Journal of Accounting, Auditing & Finance*. 35, no. 3, 471–500. doi:10.1177/0148558X17748277

Johnston, A. 2018. "Trends in Manufacturing Inventory Efficiency: 1980–2013." *Atlantic Marketing Journal* 7, no. 2, ISSN: 2165–3887.

Jong, P., S. Elfayoumy, and O. Schnusenberg. 2017. "From Returns to Tweets and Back: An Investigation of the Stocks in the Dow Jones Industrial Average." *Journal of Behavioral Finance* 18, no. 1, 54–64. doi:10.1080/15427560.201 7.1276066

Jovanovic, F. 2018. "A Comparison Between Qualitative and Quantitative Histories: The Example of the Efficient Market Hypothesis." *Journal of Economic Methodology* 25, no. 4, 291–310. doi:10.1080/1350178X.2018.1529135

Junaid, S., and T. Ali. 2020. "Impact of Asset Utilization and Finance Expenses on Profitability of the Textile Industry of Pakistan." *Journal of Finance, Accounting and Management* 11, no. 2, pp. 59–70.

Junaid, T., and K. Ali. July 2020. "Impact of Asset Utilization and Finance Expenses on Profitability of the Textile Industry of Pakistan." *Journal of Finance, Accounting and Management* 11, no. 2, pp. 59–70.

Kaizoji, T., and M. Miyano. 2019. "Stock Market Crash of 2008: An Empirical Study of the Deviation of Share Prices from Company Fundamentals." *Applied Economics Letters* 26, no. 5, 362–369. doi:10.1080/13504851.2018.1486004

Kaplan, M., and M. Haenlein. 2019. "Siri, Siri, in My Hand: Who's the Fairest in the Land? On the Interpretations, Illustrations, and Implications of Artificial Intelligence." *Business Horizons* 62, no. 1, pp. 15–25.

Kaplan, R., and J. Bruns. 1987. *Accounting and Management: A Field Study Perspective.* Boston, MA: Harvard Business School Press.

Kaplan, R.E., and D.P. Norton. 1992. "The Balanced Scorecard—Measures That Drive Performance." *Harvard Business Review.*

Kaur, M., and R. Kaur. November 2013. "Kaizen Costing Technique – A Literature Review." *International Journal of Research In Commerce & Management* 4, no. 11, ISSN: 0976–2183.

Kaushik, N., and S. Chauhan. January 2019. "The Role of Financial Constraints in the Relationship Between Working Capital Management and Firm Performance." *IUP Journal of Applied Finance.* 25, no. 1, pp. 60–82.

Keil, J., and K. Muller. June 2020. "Bank Branching Deregulation and the Syndicated Loan Market." *Journal of Financial and Quantitative Analysis* 55, no. 4, 1269–1303. doi:10.1017/S0022109019000607

Kelley, E., and P. Tetlock. March 2017. "Retail Short Selling and Stock Prices." *Review of Financial Studies* 30, no. 3, 801–834. doi:10.1093/rfs/hhw089

Kelly, S. 2019. "SEC V. Creditors: Why Sec Civil Enforcement Practice Demonstrates the Need for a Reprioritization Of Securities Fraud Claims In Bankruptcy." *St. John's Law Review* 92, no. 915, pp. 915–941.

Kern, D. April 2015. "Tax Loss Harvesting: Beware of Unrealistic Expectations." *Investment Advisor* 35, no. 4, pp. 40–42.

Kesavan, S., V. Gaur, and A. Ananth Raman. 2010. "Do Inventory and Gross Margin Data Improve Sales Forecasts for U.S. Public Retailers?" *Management Science* 56, no 9, pp. 1519–1533.

Khokhar, A. 2019. *"Working Capital Investment: A Comparative Study - Canada Versus the United States." Multinational Finance Journal* 23, nos 1–2, pp. 65–102, 38.

KiHoon, H., P. Kyounghoon, and Y. Jongmin. 2018. "Crowding Out in a Dual Currency Regime? Digital Versus Fiat Currency." *Emerging Markets Finance & Trade* 54, 2495–2515, 1540-496X print/1558-0938. online doi:10.1080/1540496X.2018.1452732

Kim, Y.R. September 2019. "Does aid for Trade Diversify the Export Structure of Recipient Countries?" *World Economy* 42, no. 9, 2684–2722. doi:10.1111/twec.12845

Kinsella, M. December 2017. "Hostile Takeovers-An Analysis Through Just War Theory." *Journal of Business Ethics* 146, no. 4, 771–786. doi:10.1007/s10551-016-3256-x

Kirkby, R. 2018. "Cryptocurrencies and Digital Fiat Currencies." *The Australian Economic Review*, 51, no. 4, 527–539. doi:10.1111/1467-8462.12307

Kitts, I.T. 2020. "Between Cylla and Charybdis Maritime Liens and the Bankruptcy Code." *Brooklyn Journal of Corporate, Financial & Commercial Law* 14, no. 1, 125–147.

Klebanov, B. Winter 2019. "Expected Rate of Return of Investments with Uncertain Timing." *The Journal of Performance Measurement. Market Reaction to Goodwill Impairments*, pp. 28–39.

Knauer, T., and A. Wöhrmann. September 2016. "Market Reaction to Goodwill Impairments." *European Accounting Review* 25, no. 3, 421–49. doi:10.1080/09638180.2015.1042888.

Knauer, T., and K. Möslang. 2018. "The Adoption and Benefits of Life Cycle Costing." *Journal of Accounting & Organizational Change* 14, no. 2, 188–215. doi:10.1108/JAOC-04-2016-0027

Korkmaz, Ö. 2017. "Is Minsky's Instability Hypothesis Acceptable for the Relation Between Borrowing Rate And Profitability?" *Financial Studies* 21 no 1, 6–27.

Kormendi, R. December 1983. *"Government Debt, Government Spending, and Private Sector Behavior." American Economic Review* 73, no. 5, p. 994.

Kraft, P. March 2015. "Rating Agency Adjustments to GAAP Financial Statements and Their Effect on Ratings and Credit Spreads." *Accounting Review* 90, no. 2, 641–674. doi:10.2308/accr-50858

Krzywdzinski, M. November 2017. "Automation, Skill Requirements and Labour Use Strategies: High-Wage and Low-Wage Approaches to High-Tech Manufacturing in the Automotive Industry." *New Technology, Work & Employment* 32, no. 3, 247–267. doi:10.1111/ntwe.12100

Kubálek, J., Z. Fišerová, and M. Paseková. May 2019. "Debtor Path to Bankruptcy: Dependence on the Annual Percentage Rate Charge." *International Advances in Economic Research* 25, no. 2, 247–248. doi:10.1007/s11294-019-09728-5

Kulesza, M.G., P.Q. Weaver, and S. Friedman. 2011. "Taylor's Presence in 21st Century Management Accounting Systems and Work Process Theories." *Journal of Business & Management* 17, no. 1, pp. 105–119.

Kumar, P., and A. Zattoni. 2019. "Farewell Editorial: Exiting Editors' Perspective on Current and Future Challenges in Corporate Governance Research." *Corp Govern Int Rev* 27, pp. 2–11.

Kuruvilla, S. 2018. "Theory of Constraints and the Thinking Process." *International Journal of Business Insights & Transformation* 11, no. 1, 10–14.

Laing, G.K., and R.W. Perrin. December 2018. *"Management Accounting in the Australian Printing Industry: A Survey." Journal of New Business Ideas & Trends.* 16, no. 3, pp. 13–9.

Landsman, W.R. 2007. "Is Fair Value Information Relevant and Reliable." *Accounting & Business Research*, 19–30, Wolters Kluwer UK.

Lee, J.B., J.J. Reeves, A.C. Tjahja, and X. Xie. March 2019. "Targeting Market Neutrality." *Quantitative Finance* 19, no. 3, 437–451. doi:10.1080/146976 88.2018.1479066

Lemons, D. January 2012. "When to Start Collecting Social Security Benefits: A Break-Even Analysis." *Journal of Financial Planning*, pp. 52–60.

Lettau, M., and A. Madhavan. 2018. "Exchange-Traded Funds 101 for Economists." *Journal of Economic Perspectives* 32. no. 1, 135–154. doi:10.1257/jep.32.1.135

Levin, M.B., A.A. Mingione, and S.E. Tisman. Winter 2019. "New York Closes in on Comprehensive Employee Wage Lien Law." *Employee Relations Law Journal* 45, no. 3, pp. 26–28.

Levitin, A.J. January 2018. "Pandora's Digital Box: The Promise and Perils of Digital Wallets." *University of Pennsylvania Law Review* 166, no. 2, pp. 305–376.

Li, X., N. Rafaliya, M.F. Baki, and B.A. Chaouch. 2017. "Scheduling Elective Surgeries: The Tradeoff Among Bed Capacity, Waiting Patients and Operating Room Utilization Using Goal Programming." *Health Care Management Science* 20, 33–54. doi:10.1007/s10729-015-9334-2

Lian, C., Y. Ma., and C. Wang. June 2019 "Low Interest Rates and Risk-Taking: Evidence from Individual Investment Decisions." *Review of Financial Studies* 32, no 6, 2107–2148. doi:10.1093/rfs/hhy111

Lifland, S. 2010. "The Corporate Soap-Opera "As the Cash Turns": Management of Working Capital and Potential External Financing Needs." *Review of Business* 32, no. 1, pp. 35–46.

Lowry, M., M. Rossi, and Z. Zhu. February 2019. "Informed Trading by Advisor Banks: Evidence from Options Holdings." *Review of Financial Studies* 32, no. 2, 605–645. doi:10.1093/rfs/hhy072

Luther, J. March 2020. "Twenty-First Century Financial Regulation: P2p Lending, Fintech, And The Argument For A Special Purpose Fintech Charter Approach." *University of Pennsylvania Law Review* 168, no. 4, pp. 1013–1059.

MacGillivray, B.H. July 2019. "Null Hypothesis Testing Scientific Inference: A Critique of the Shaky Premise at the Heart of the Science and Values Debate, and a Defense of Value-Neutral Risk Assessment." *Risk Analysis: An International Journal* 39, no. 7, 1520–1532. doi:10.1111/risa.13284

Mack, E., T.H. Grubesic, and E. Kessler. September 2007. "Indices of Industrial Diversity and Regional Economic Composition." *Growth and Change* 38, no. 3, pp. 474–509.

Mackey, J.B. June 2019. "Can We Better Understand Markets with a Four-Environment Perspective?" *Journal of Financial Planning* 32, no. 6, pp. 34–38.

Magnus, S.M., and A. Rudra. 2019. "Operationally Intuitive Logistics Dashboards for Supply Chain Management in Oil and Gas Based on Human Cognition." *Journal of Management Policy and Practice* 20, no. 4, pp. 78–84.

Manapat, R.K.S., and V.G. Sridharan. 2020. "The Role of Strategic Cost Management in Marketing Decisions: A Case Evidence of Brand Acquisition Assessment." *Management Accounting Frontiers* 3, pp. 5–24.

Mandel, G.N., K.R. Olson, and A.A. Fast. 2020. "Debunking Intellectual Property Myths: Cross-Cultural Experiments on Perceptions of Property." *Brigham Young University Law Review*, no. 2, pp. 219–273.

Masiak, C., J.H. Block, T. Masiak., M. Neuenkirch, and K.N. Pielen. December 2020. "Initial Coin Offerings (ICOs): Market Cycles and Relationship with Bitcoin and Ether." *Small Business Economics* 55, no. 4, pp. 1113–1130.

Matanova, N., T. Steigner., B. Yi, and Q. Zheng. July 2019. "Going Concern Opinions and IPO Pricing Accuracy." *Review of Quantitative Finance & Accounting* 53, no. 1, 195–238. doi:10.1007/s11156-018-0747-0

Mawanga, F. 2017. "Investigating A Random Walk In Air Cargo Exports Of Fresh Agricultural Products: Evidence From A Developing Country." *Studies Business and Economics* 12, no. 1, 129–140. doi:10.1515/sbe-2017-0010

May 2016. "Earnings-Per-Share Standard Gets Positive Feedback." *Journal of Accountancy*. p. 11.

McBride, K., T. Hines, and R. Craig. September 2016. "A Rum Deal: The Purser's Measure and Accounting Control of Materials in the Royal Navy. 1665–1832" *Business History* 58, no 6, 925–946. doi:10.1080/00076791.2 016.1153068

McCormack, J.L. Winter 2018. "A Message from the Editor." *Journal of Applied Corporate Finance* 30, no. 1.

McCoy, C., and H. Rosenbaum. 2019. "Uncovering Unintended and Shadow Practices of Users of Decision Support System Dashboards in Higher Education Institutions." *Journal of The Association For Information Science And Technology* 70, no. 4, 370–384.

McCunn, P. December 1998. "The Balanced Scorecard…The Eleventh Commandment." *Management Accounting* 76, no. 11, p. 34.

McInnis. J., Y. Yu., and C. Yust. November 2018. "Does Fair Value Accounting Provide More Useful Financial Statements than Current GAAP for Banks?" *The Accounting Review American Accounting Association* 93, no. 6, 257–279. doi:10.2308/accr-52007

Meisel, S. (undated). "Literature Review of Earnings Management – 1985–2014." *Franklin Business & Law Journal.* 91–143. www.moreheadstate.edu/content

Mikalef, P., I. Pappas., J. Krogstie., and M. Giannakos. 2018. "Big Data Analytics Capabilities: A Systematic Literature Review and Research Agenda." *Inf Syst E-Bus Manage* 16, 547–578. doi:10.1007/s10257-017-0362-y 547-578

Miller, R.A. January 2018. "Minsky's Financial Instability Hypothesis and the Role of Equity: The Accounting Behind Hedge, Speculative, and Ponzi Finance." *Journal of Post Keynesian Economics* 41, no. 1, 126–138. doi:10.10 80/01603477.2017.1392870

Minsky, H. 1992. "The Financial Instability Hypothesis." Working Paper No. 74. New York, NY: Levy Economics Institute.

Mitra, S., T. Al-Hayale, and M. Hossain. 2019. "Does late 10K filing Impact Companies' Financial Reporting Strategy? Evidence from Discretionary Accruals and Real Transaction Management." *Journal of Business Finance & Accounting* 46, nos. 5–6, 569–607. doi:10.1111/jbfa.12369

Moily, J.P. November 2015. "Economic Manufacturing Quantity and Its Integrating Implications." *Production & Operations Management* 24, no. 11, 1696–1705. doi.10.1111/poms.12411

Moosa, I. June 2010. "Some Pedagogical Pitfalls in the Definitions of Arbitrage, Hedging and Speculation." *Banking & Finance Review* 2, no. 1, pp. 87–94.

Morales-Díaz, J., and C. Zamora-Ramírez. 2018. "The Impact of IFRS 16 on Key Financial Ratios: A New Methodological Approach." *Accounting in Europe* 15, no. 1, 105–133. doi:10.1080/17449480.2018.1433307

Murphy, M. 2020. "Hedge Accounting may be More Beneficial After FASB's Changes." *Association of International Certified Professional Accountants.* Ellen. Goldstein@aicpa-cima.com

Murphy, M.L. 2020. "Hedge Accounting May Be More Beneficial After FASB's Changes." *Journal of Accountancy* 229, no. 6, pp. 1–7.

Muthusamy, A., and S. Karthika. September 2019. "Financial Performance of Selected Cement Companies in India." *International Journal of Research in Commerce & Management* 10, no. 9, pp. 1–5.

Nagaraj, P., and C. Zhang. August 2019. "Regulatory Quality, Financial Integration and Equity Cost of Capital." *Review of International Economics* 27, no. 3, 916–935.

Nakamoto, S. 2014. "Bitcoin: A Peer-To-Peer Electronic Cash System." http://fastbull.dl.sourceforge.net/project/bitcoin/Design/%20Paper/bitcoin.pdf

Nation, F., D. Williams, and M. Buxton. 2019. "Relationship Between Audit Manager Experience and Compliance Audit Outcomes." *Journal of Accounting and Finance* 19, no. 5, pp. 101–111.

Nezlobin, A., M. Rajan, and S. Reichelstein. June 2016. "Structural Properties of the Price-to-Earnings and Price-To-Book Ratios." *Review of Accounting Studies* 21 no. 2, 438–472. doi:10.1007/s11142-016-9356-0

Nichita, E. 2019. "Intangible Assets – Insights from a Literature Review." *Accounting and Management Information Systems* 18, no. 2, pp. 224–261.

Noailly, J., J.C. van den Bergh, and C.A. Withagen. 2003. "Evolution of Harvesting Strategies: Replicator and Resource Dynamics." *Journal of Evolutionary Economics* 13, no. 2, 183. doi:10.1007/s00191-003-0146-z

O'Sullivan, P. 2018. "The Capital Asset Pricing Model and the Efficient Markets Hypothesis: The Compelling Fairy Tale of Contemporary Financial Economics." *International Journal of Political Economy* 47, 225–252, LLC ISSN: 0891-1916 print/1558-0970. online doi:10.1080/08911916.2018.1517462

Obaidat. A.N. Spring 2019. "Is Economic Value Added Superior To Earnings And Cash Flows In Explaining Market Value Added? An Empirical Study." *International Journal of Business, Accounting, and Finance* 13, no 1, pp. 57–69.

Obaidat, A.N. Spring 2018. "Does Income Smoothing Affect Stock Market Price Volatility? An Empirical Study." *International Journal of Business, Accounting, and Finance* 12, no. 1, pp. 29–41

Oliver, M., and J. Rutterford. Summer 2020. 'The Capital Market is Dead': The Difficult Birth of Index-Linked Gilts in the UK." *Economic History Review* 73, no. 1, 258–280.

Olson, G.T., and M.S. Pagano. 2017. "The Empirical Average Cost of Capital: A New Approach to Estimating the Cost of Corporate Funds." *Journal of Applied Corporate Finance* 29, no. 3, pp. 101–111.

Om Sai Ram Centre for Financial Management Research. 2015. "Financial Management Indicators To Aid Decision Making." *Journal of Financial Management and Analysis* 28, no. 2, pp. v–xvi.

Omar, A., and A.P. Tang. September 2019. "Earnings Management and Convertible Preferred Stock." *International Review of Economics & Finance* 63, 423–443.

Ortner, D. 2015. "Cybercrime and Punishment: The Russian Mafia and Russian Responsibility to Exercise Due Diligence to Prevent Trans-boundary Cybercrime." *Brigham Young University Law Review*, pp. 177–216.

Özera, G., and E. Yılmaz. 2011. "Effects of Procedural Justice Perception, Budgetary Control Effectiveness and Ethical Work Climate on Propensity to Create Budgetary Slack." *Business and Economics Research Journal* 2, no. 4, 1–18. ISSN: 1309-2448.

Pacheco-Paredes, A.A., D.V. Rama, and C.M. Wheatley. 2017. "The Timing of Auditor Hiring: Determinants and Consequences." *Accounting Horizons American Accounting Association* 31, no. 3, 85–10. doi:10.2308/acch-51732 3

Paek, J.H. 2000. "Running A Profitable Construction Company: Revisited Break-Even Analysis." *Journal of Management in Engineering*, pp. 40–46.

Parks, L. 2019. "Our Enduring Legacy: The History of the IMA." *Strategic Finance* 100, no. 12, pp. 28–31.

Pasztor, J. March 2018. "Bitcoin Investing—An Ethical and Regulatory Quandary." *Journal of Financial Service Professionals*, pp. 30–33.

Patin, J., M. Rahman, and M. Mustafa. 2020. "Impact of Total Asset Turnover Ratios on Equity Returns: Dynamic Panel Data." *Analyses Journal of Accounting, Business and Management* (JABM) 27, no. 1, pp. 19–29.

Pelz, M. 2019. "Can Management Accounting Be Helpful for Young and Small Companies? Systematic Review of a Paradox." *International Journal of Management Reviews* 21, 256–274. doi:10.1111/ijmr.12197

Pennacchi, G., T. Vermaelen, and C.C. Wolff. June 2014. "Contingent Capital: The Case of COERCs." *Journal of Financial & Quantitative Analysis* 49, no. 3, 541–574. doi:10.1017/S0022109014000398

Peterson, J. February 2016. "Audit Quality and the Expectations Gap It's Time for a Model that Fits the Data." *The CPA Journal*, pp. 6–9.

Peterson, R.L., C.K. Ma, and R.J. Ritchey. August 1992. "Dependence in Commodity Prices." *Journal of Futures Markets* 12, no. 4, 429–446. doi:10.1002/fut.3990120405

Phan, T.N., K. Baird, and B. Blair. 2014. "The Use and Success of Activity-Based Management Practices at Different Organisational Life Cycle Stages." *International Journal of Production Research* 52, no. 3, 787–803. doi:10.1080/00207543.2013.839893

Phillips, F., and L. Heiser. 2011. "A Field Experiment Examining the Effects of Accounting Equation Emphasis and Transaction Scope on Students Learning to Journalize." *Issues In Accounting Education.* 26, no. 4, 681–99. doi:10.2308/iace-50051

Pieters, M. 2019. "International Code of Ethics for Professional Accountants: A Behind the Scenes Look at the eCode." *Australian Accounting Review* 29, no. 3, pp. 595–598.

Poudel, R, D. Prasad., and R. Jain. 2020. "The Altman 'Z' is "50" and Still Young: Bankruptcy Prediction and Stock Market Reaction due to Sudden Exogenous Shock." *Journal of Accounting and Finance* 20, no. 2, pp. 65–73.

Prada, G. June 2008. "Exploring Technological Innovation in Health Systems: Is Canada Measuring Up?" *Journal of Management & Marketing in Healthcare* 1, J62–Î74.

Prahalad, C.K., and G. Hamel. 1990. "The Core Competence of the Corporation." *Harvard Business Review* 68, no. 3, 79–91.

Prasad, A., and L. Warrier. 2016. "Mr. Porter and the New World of Increasing Returns to Scale." *Journal of Management Research* 16, no. 1, pp. 3–15.

Preusch, N. June 2015. "Exercising Due Diligence." *Journal of Accountancy* 219, no. 6, pp. 1–3.

Prober, L., I. Mericand, and G. Meric. 2016. "A Comparison of the Financial Characteristics of U.S. and U.K. Manufacturing Firms." *Quarterly Journal of Finance & Accounting* 54, nos. 3–4, pp. 1–14.

Qi, H., and Y. Xie. August 2016. "Cost of Capital: Spot Rate or Forward Rate?" *Applied Economics* 48, no. 40, 3804–3811. doi:10.1080/00036846.2016.11 45350

Raguseo, E., and C. Vitari. August 2018. "Investments in Big Data Analytics and Firm Performance: An Empirical Investigation of Direct and Mediating Effects." *International Journal of Production Research* 56, no. 15, 5206–5221. doi:10.1080/00207543.2018.1427900

Rahman, M.T., and S.Z. Hossain. 2020. "Company-Specific Characteristics and Market-driven Fixed Asset Revaluation in an Emerging Asian Economy." *Management & Accounting Review* 19, no. 3, pp. 151–184.

Raj, M., and R. Seamans. 2019. "Primer on Artificial Intelligence and Robotics." *Journal of Organization Design* 8, no. 1, 1–14. doi:10.1186/s41469-019-0050-0

Ramesh, K., and T.R. Annamalai. Spring 2020. "Corporate Tax Havens and Venture Capital Investment." *Journal of Taxation of Investments* 37, no. 3, pp. 79–91.

Rankin, R. 2020. "The Predictive Impact of Contextual Factors on Activity-based Costing Adoption." *Journal of Accounting and Finance* 20, no. 1, pp. 66–81.

Rashty, J. May 2012. "Employee Stock Purchase Plans and the Calculation of Basic and Diluted Earnings per Share." *Accounting and Auditing Journal*, 32–36.

Roberts, J., and J. Karras. Fall 2019. "What is Blockchain?" *Economic Development Journal* 18, no, 4, pp. 5–10.

Rottkamp, D.M. April 2019. "The Reporting Impact of ASU 2016-14." *CPA Journal* 89, no. 4, pp. 40–45.

Russon, M.G., and V. Bansal. 2016. "An Improved Methodology to Assess Value-relevance of Earnings and Book Values on Corporate Equity Securities." *Journal of Accounting and Finance* 16. no. 2, pp. 117–128.

Ryan, J., M. Ives, and I. Dunham. 2019. "The Impact of Cost of Capital Reductions on Regulated Water Utilities in England and Wales: An Analysis of Isomorphism and Stakeholder Outcomes." *Journal of Management & Governance* 23, no. 1, 259–287. doi:10.1007/s10997-018-9427-7

Ryu, D., and H. Yang. December 2018. "The Directional Information Content of Options Volumes." *Journal of Futures Markets* 38, no. 12, 1533–1548. doi:10.1002/fut.21960

Sabia, J. October 2015. "Minimum Wages and Gross Domestic Product." *Contemporary Economic Policy* (ISSN 1465-7287) 33, no. 4, 587–605. doi:10.1111/coep.12099

Safari, A. June 2017. "Worldwide Venture Capital, Intellectual Property Rights, and Innovation." *Industrial & Corporate Change* 26, no. 3, 485–515.

Saibeni, A. November 2018. "Mortgage Amortization Revisited: An Alternative Methodology." *The CPA Journal*, pp. 54–59.

Said, H. Fall 2016. "Using Different Probability Distributions For Managerial Accounting Technique: The Cost-Volume-Profit Analysis." *Journal of Business and Accounting* 9, no. 1, pp. 3–24.

Saltaji, I.M.F. June 2018. "Corporate Governance: A General." *Review Internal Auditing & Risk Management* 13, no. 1, pp. 56–63.

Salvador, E., and V. Aragó. 2014. "Measuring Hedging Effectiveness of Index Futures Contracts: Do Dynamic Models Outperform Static Models? A Regime-Switching Approach Enrique." *The Journal of Futures Markets* 34, no. 4, 374–398, doi:10.1002/fut.21598

Sanchez-Medina1, A.J., F. Blazquez-Santana, and B. Alonso Jesu´s. 2019. "Do Auditors Reflect the True Image of the Company Contrary to the Clients' Interests? An Artificial Intelligence Approach." *J Bus Ethics* 155, 529–545 doi:10.1007/s10551-017-3496-4

Sangster, A. March 2018. "Pacioli's Lens: God, Humanism, Euclid, and the Rhetoric of Double Entry." *The Accounting Review* American Accounting Association 93, no. 2, 299–314. doi:10.2308/accr-51850

Sangster, A., and G. Scataglinibelghitar. 2010. "Luca Pacioli: The Father of Accounting Education." *Accounting Education* 19, no. 4, pp. 423–428.

Scheck, H.A. February 14, 2020. "SEC Is Watching Earnings Management Disclosures." *Blumberg Law.* https://news.bloomberglaw.com/securities-law/insight-sec-is-watching-earnings-management-disclosures

Schmutte, J., R. James, and J.R. Duncan. August 2019. "The Statement of Cash Flows Turns 30 - Common Reporting Deficiencies and Recent Changes." *The CPA Journal*, 6–10.

Scholl, W., and C. Schermuly. 2020. "The Impact of Culture on Corruption, Gross Domestic Product, and Human Development." *Journal of Business Ethics*, pp. 171–189. doi:10.1007/s10551-018-3977-0

Schweikart, J.A. May 1992. "Cognitive-Contingency Theory and the Study of Ethics in Accounting." *Journal of Business Ethics* 11, nos. 5–6, 471–478. doi:10.1007/BF00870558

Secrest, T.W. Fall 2020. "Observations Regarding Yield Curve Inversions." *Journal of Business & Behavioral Sciences* 32, no. 2, 143–155.

Sengupta, P., and Z. Wang. September 2011. "Pricing of Off-Balance Sheet Debt: How do Bond Market Participants Use the Footnote Disclosures on Operating Leases and Postretirement Benefit Plans?" *Accounting & Finance* 51, no. 3, 787–808. doi:10.1111/j.1467-629X.2010.00368

Shekarian, E., E. Olugu., S. Abdul-Rashid, and N. Kazemi. 2016. "An Economic Order Quantity Model Considering Different Holding Costs for Imperfect Quality Items Subject to Fuzziness and Learning." *Journal of Intelligent & Fuzzy Systems* 30, 2985–2997. doi:10.3233/IFS-151907 IOS Press

Shelton, S., and O. Whittington. January 2008. "The Influence of the Auditor's Report on Investors' Evaluations After the Sarbanes-Oxley Act." *Managerial Auditing Journal* 23, no. 2, pp. 142–160.

Sheraz, M., and S. Dedu. 2020. "Bitcoin Cash: Stochastic Models of Fat-Tail Returns And Risk Modeling." *Economic Computation & Economic Cybernetics Studies & Research* 54, no. 3, 43–58. doi:10.24818/18423264/54.3.20.03

Futagami, S., and M.M. Helms. Spring 2017. "Can Women Avoid the Rice Paper Ceiling? A SWOT Analysis of Entrepreneurship in Japan." *SAM Advanced Management Journal (07497075)* 82, no. 2, pp. 40–52.

Siering, M. March 2019. "The Economics of Stock Touting During Internet-Based Pump and Dump Campaigns." *Information Systems Journal* 29, no. 2, 456–483. doi:10.1111/isj.12216

Singh, G., and M. Shaik. February 2021. "The Short-Term Impact of COVID-19 on Global Stock Market Indices Contemporary Economics." 15, no. 1, 1–18.

Sinkin, J., and T. Putney. December 2017. "Mergers and Acquisitions of Accounting Firms." *CPA Journal*, pp. 30–36.

Sinkin, J., and T. Putney. December 2017. "Mergers and Acquisitions of Accounting Firms." *CPA Journal* 87, no. 12, pp. 30–35.

Skarlatos, B.C., and D. Plum. 2018. "The IRS Is Zeroing in on Failure to Report Crypto Currency: But Are Penalties Really Appropriate?" *Journal of Tax Practice & Procedure* 20, no. 1, pp. 19–51.

Slack, R., and D. Cambell. 2016. "Meeting Users' Information Needs: The Use and Usefulness of Integrated Reporting." *Association of Certified Chartered Accountants Journal*

Smith, B. October 2016. "The Merits and Downsides of Preferred Shares." *Benefits Canada* 40, no. 9.

Smith, C., and A. Kumar. December 2018. "Crypto-Currencies – An Introduction To Not-So-Funny." *Journal of Economic Surveys* 32, no. 5, 1531–1559. 3 Diagrams, 2 Charts, 3 Graphs. doi:10.1111/joes.12289

Soldić-Aleksić J., B. Chroneos-Krasavac, and E. Karamata. 2020. "Business Analytics: New Concepts and Trends. Management." *Journal of Sustainable Business and Management Solutions in Emerging Economies* 25. no. 2.

Spiotto, J.E. Winter 2019. "The History and Justification for Timely Payment of Statutory Liens and Pledged Special Revenues Bond Financing in a Chapter 9 Municipal Debt Adjustment Proceeding: Is a Model State Law Necessary or Required?" *Municipal Finance Journal* 39, no. 4, pp. 47–97.

Sriananthakumar, S. 2019. "Using Point Optimal Test of a Simple Null Hypothesis for Testing a Composite Null Hypothesis Via Maximized Monte Carlo Approach." *Econometric Reviews* 38, no. 4, 451–464. doi:10.1080/074 74938.2017.1382781

Steen, A., and D. Welch. September 2011. "Are Accounting Metrics Applicable to Human Resources? The Case of Return on Investment in Valuing International Assignments." *Australasian Accounting Business & Finance Journal* 5, no. 3, pp. 57–72.

Stepien, K. 2015. "Estimated Values: The Provisions and Write Down of Assets as Tools to Manipulate Financial Results of Enterprises." *Copernican Journal of Finance and Accounting* 4, no. 1, pp. 157–171.

Stowe, D.L., and J.D. Stowe. 2018. "Financial Markets, Institutions & Instruments." *wileyonlinelibrary*.com/journal/fmii, 169–186. doi:10.1111/fmii.12102

Stuart, R. 2020. "U.S. GAAP vs. IFRS: Contingencies and Provisions." National Professional Standards Group, RSM US LLP. richard.stuart@rsmus.com

Stunda, R.A. Fall 2017. "Reporting of Cash Flows Under International Financial Reporting Standards Versus Generally Accepted Accounting Principles and the Effect on Security Prices." *International Journal of Business, Accounting, and Finance* 11, no. 2, pp. 63–74.

Susarla, A., and T. Mukhopadhyay. September 2019. "Can Outsourcing of Information Technology Foster Innovations In Client Organizations? An Empirical Analysis." *MIS Quarterly* 43, no. 3, 929–949. doi:10.25300/MISQ/2019/13535 2019

Syed Nor, S.H., S. Ismail, and B.W. Yap. 2019. "Personal Bankruptcy Prediction Using Decision Tree Model." *Journal of Economics, Finance and Administrative Science* 24, no. 47, 157–170 doi:10.1108/JEFAS-08-2018-0076

Szu, Wen-Ming; Y., C. Wang, and W.R. Yang. June 2015 *Review of Pacific Basin Financial Markets & Policies* 18, no. 2, 1–35. doi:10.1142/S0219091515500101

Taggart, H. July 1953. "Sacred Cows in Accounting." *The Accounting Review*. 315–316.

Tang, Z., G. Srivastava, and S. Liu. 2020. "Swarm Intelligence and Ant Colony Optimization in Accounting Model Choices." *Journal of Intelligent & Fuzzy Systems* 38, no. 3, 2415–2423. doi:10.3233/JIFS-179530

Tanner, E.C. 2019. "Disinflation, External Vulnerability, and Fiscal Intransigence: Some Unpleasant Mundellian Arithmetic." *Journal of Applied Economics* 22, no. 1, 403–436. doi:10.1080/15140326.2019.1644718

Taylor III, L.J., A.M. Nunley III, and M.D. Flock. August 2004. "WIP Inventory: Asset or Liability?" *Cost Engineering* 46, no. 8, pp. 19–25.

Taylor J., J. Vithayathil, and D. Yim. September/October 2018. "Are Corporate Social Responsibility (CSR) Initiatives Such As Sustainable Development and Environmental Policies Value Enhancing or Window Dressing?" *Corporate Social Responsibility & Environmental Management* 25, no. 5, pp. 971–980. doi:10.1002/esr.1513

Tesfaselassie, M.F. October 2019. "The Real Effects of Credible Disinflation in the Presence of Real Wage Rigidities." *Economica* 86, no. 344, 728–749. doi:10.1111/ecca.12288

The Cost of Capital. September 2020. *International Accountant* 113, 8–11.

Thukral, S. February 2017. "Unfolding Bitcoin." *CLEAR International Journal of Research in Commerce & Management* 8, no. 2, pp. 32–33.

Toemer, M.D. February 2009. "A Guide to Using the Accounting Standards Codification." *The CPA Journal*, 200–10. doi:1142/S0219091515500101.5

Toumeh, A., Y. Sofri, and W. Siam. 2018. "Expectations Gap Between Auditors and User of Financial Statements in the Audit Process: An Auditors' Perspective." *Asia-Pacific Management Accounting Journal* 13, no. 3, pp. 103–136.

Trainor, J.E., C.R. Phillips and M. Cangialosi. 2018. "An Analysis of the FASB's New Going-Concern Standard and Its Relation to Liquidation Basis Accounting Requirements Review of Business." *Interdisciplinary Journal on Risk and Society* 38, no. 1, pp. 16–35.

Tricker, P.C. July 2018. "Annuities and Moral Hazard: Can Longevity Insurance Increase Longevity?" *Journal of Financial Service Professionals*, pp. 43–50.

Troncoso, J.N. 2019. "Time traders: Derivatives, Minsky and a Reinterpretation of the Causes of the 2008 Global Financial Crisis." *Journal of Post Keynesian Economics* 42, no. 3, 469–486. doi:10.1080/01603477.2018.1533414

Tuin, R. October 2020. "Flawless Start-up of Production Plants in Process Industries: The Link between Successful Project Performance and Optimal Future Operations." *Journal of Business Chemistry*, 32–58. doi:10.17879/60119502196

Unsal, O., and B. Rayfield. April, 2020. "Correction To: Corporate Governance and Employee Treatment: Evidence from Takeover Defenses." *Journal of Economics & Finance* 44, no. 2, 392–416. doi:10.1007/s12197-019-09486-4

Vega-Mejía, C.A. J.R. Montoya-Torres, and S.M.N. Islam. 2019. "Consideration of Triple Bottom Line Objectives for Sustainability in the Optimization of Vehicle Routing and Loading Operations: A Systematic Literature Review." *Annals of Operations Research* 273, 311–375. https://doi.org/10.1007/s10479-017-2723-9

Vincent, N.E., and A.M. Wilkins. Spring 2020. "Challenges When Auditing Cryptocurrencies." *Current Issues in Auditing American Accounting Association* 14, no. 1, A46–A58. doi:10.2308/ciia-52675

Violet, W., and J.D. Hansen. October 2013. "Abstractions in Accounting (The Accounting Problem)." *The Journal of Theoretical Accounting Research* 1, no. 9, 108–114.

Vogiazas, S., and C. Alexiou. February 2019. "Bitcoin: The Road to Hell Is Paved With Good Promises." *Economic Notes* 48, no. 1. doi: 10.1111/ecno.12119

Volmers, G., V. Antonelli, R. D'Allesio, and R. Rossi. 2016. "Cost Accounting for War: Contracting Procedures and Cost-plus Pricing in WWI Industrial Mobilization in Italy." *European Accounting Review* 25, no. 4, 735–769. doi: 10.1080/09638180.2015.1085887

Walton, P. August 2018. "Discussion of Barker and Teixeira. Gaps in the IFRS Conceptual Framework. Accounting in Europe, 15) and Van Mourik and Katsuo ([2018]. Profit or loss in the IASB Conceptual Framework." *Accounting in Europe* 15, no. 2, 193–199. doi:10.1080/17449480.2018.1437457

Wampler, B., and C. Smolinski. Spring 2018. "Classification of Cash Flows By Issuers of Debt Instruments." *Journal of Theoretical Accounting Research* 13, no. 2, pp. 33–46.

Wang, Y., C. Wu, and L. Yang. December 2015. "Hedging with Futures: Does Anything Beat the Naïve Hedging Strategy?" *Management Science* 61, no. 12, 2870–2889, ISSN 0025-1909 (print) ISSN 1526-5501.

Ward, C.L., and S.K. Lowe. Spring 2017. "Cultural Impact of International Financial Reporting Standards on The Comparability of Financial Statements." *International Journal of Business, Accounting, & Finance* 11, no. 1, pp. 46–56.

Watts, J. 2018. "Trend Spotting: Using Text Analysis to Model Market Dynamics International." *Journal of Market Research* 60, no. 4, 408–418. doi:10.1177/1470785318758558

Weber, R. November 2018. "An Advisor's Introduction to Blockchain." *Journal of Financial Service Professionals*, pp. 49–53.

Wegmann, G. 2019. *Asia-Pacific Management Accounting Journal* 14, no. 2, pp. 161–184.

Wegren, S.K., A.M. Nikulin, and I. Trotsuk. July 2019. "Russian Agriculture During Putin's Fourth Term: A Swot Analysis." *Post-Communist Economies* 31, no. 4. 419–450. doi:10.1080/14631377.2019.1579892

Weinberger, A.M., and M. Murphy. Winter 2016. "Cases in Brief." *Appraisal Journal* 84, no. 1, pp. 1–10.

Weiss, L., and R. Kivetz. 2019. "Opportunity Cost Overestimation." *Journal of Marketing Research* 56, no. 3, 518–533. doi:10.1177/0022243718819474

Whitaker, A. Summer 2019. "Art and Blockchain A Primer, History, and Taxonomy of Blockchain Use Cases in the Arts Artivate:" *A Journal Of Entrepreneurship in the Arts* 8, no. 2, pp. 21–46.

White, M., I. Anitsal, and M. Anitsal. 2015. "Adoption of Activity-Based Costing: Abrahamson's Four Perspectives Model as an Illustration." *Business Studies Journal*, no. 1, pp. 66–83.

Whitfield, P. June 19, 2019. "What Is A Blue Chip Stock?" *Investors Business Daily*.

Wilbanks, D. February 2016. *Professional Safety* 61, no. 2, pp. 23–25.

Xiaoquan, J., and K. Qiang, 2020. "Cross-Sectional PEG Ratios, Market Equity Premium, and Macroeconomic Activity." *Journal of Accounting, Auditing & Finance* 35, no. 3, 471–500. doi:10.1177/0148558X17748277 journals. sagepub.com/home/JAF

Yann-Jy Yang, Y.J. and Hwang J.C. 2020. "Recent Development Trend of Blockchain Technologies: A Patent Analysis." *International Journal of Electronic Commerce Studies.* 11, no. 1, 1–12. doi:10.7903/ijecs.1931

Yao, L. 2019. "Financial Accounting Intelligence Management of Internet of Things Enterprises Based on Data Mining Algorithm." *Journal of Intelligent & Fuzzy Systems* 37, no. 5, 5915–5923. doi:10.3233/JIFS-179173

Yu, E.P.Y., C.Q. Guo, and B.V. Luu. 2018. "Environmental, social and governance transparency and firm value." *Business Strategy & the Environment* 27, no. 7, 987–1004. doi:10.1002/bse.2047

Zarb, B.J. Winter 2016. "Have Earning Power and Financial Health in the Airline Industry Improved Since the 2008–2009 Recession?" *International Journal of Business, Accounting, and Finance* 10, no. 2, pp. 56–70.

Zhang, C., M. Leng, and L. Zhou. January 2020. "Explained Using Porter's Five Forces Analysis Model: Taking Mental Challenged Car Wash As An Example." *International Journal of Organizational Innovation* 12, no. 3, pp. 50–64. Developing Strategies of Social Enterprises.

Zhang, J. July 2019. "Learning from the Current Research on Non-GAAP Financial Measures." *CPA Journal.* 89, no. 7, pp. 32–37.

Zhu, S.P., X.J. He, and X. Lu. March 2018. "A New Integral Equation Formulation for American Put Options." *Quantitative Finance* 18, no. 3, 483–490. doi:10. 1080/14697688.2017.1348617

About the Authors

Roger Hussey, PhD, MSc, FCCA, is a fellow of the Association of Chartered Certified Accountants and received his MSc in Industrial Relations and his PhD in financial communications from the University of Bath, U.K. He has taught in Australia, Canada, China, and the U.K. Roger is the author of nearly 40 books. Roger worked in industry for several years before moving to the Industrial Relations Unit at St Edmund Hall, Oxford University, as director of research into employee communications. He was later appointed as Deloitte and Touche Professor of Financial Reporting at the University of the West of England. Roger was previously Dean of the Odette School of Business and is now professor emeritus at the University of Windsor, Canada, and the University of the West of England.

Audra Ong, PhD, MBA, is a professor of accounting at the University of Windsor, Canada. She has also taught in the U.K. She received her PhD in accounting from the University of the West of England, her MBA from the University of Wales, Cardiff, and her BSc in Accounting from Queen's University, Belfast. Audra has published in academic journals and is the co-author of several books including *Strategic Cost Analysis, Pick a Number: Internationalizing U.S. Accounting,* and *Accounting for Business: Practicalities & Strategies* published by Business Expert Press.

OTHER TITLES IN THE FINANCIAL ACCOUNTING AND AUDITING COLLECTION

Mark Bettner, Bucknell University, and
Michael Coyne, Fairfield University, Editors

- *International Auditing Standards in the United States* by Asokan Anandarajan and Gary Kleinman
- *Twenty-First Century Corporate Reporting* by Gerald Trites
- *Calling Out COVID-19* by Faisal Sheikh, Nigel Iyer, Brian Leigh and Geetha Rubasundram
- *Accounting for Business* by Roger Hussey and Audra Ong
- *Tax Aspects of Corporate Division* by W. Eugene Seago
- *When Numbers Don't Add Up* by Faisal Sheikh
- *Sustainability Performance and Reporting* by Irene M. Herremans
- *Applications of Accounting Information Systems* by David M. Shapiro
- *A Non-Technical Guide to International Accounting* by Roger Hussey and Audra Ong
- *Forensic Accounting and Financial Statement Fraud, Volume I* by Zabihollah Rezaee
- *Forensic Accounting and Financial Statement Fraud, Volume II* by Zabihollah Rezaee

Concise and Applied Business Books

The Collection listed above is one of 30 business subject collections that Business Expert Press has grown to make BEP a premiere publisher of print and digital books. Our concise and applied books are for...

- Professionals and Practitioners
- Faculty who adopt our books for courses
- Librarians who know that BEP's Digital Libraries are a unique way to offer students ebooks to download, not restricted with any digital rights management
- Executive Training Course Leaders
- Business Seminar Organizers

Business Expert Press books are for anyone who needs to dig deeper on business ideas, goals, and solutions to everyday problems. Whether one print book, one ebook, or buying a digital library of 110 ebooks, we remain the affordable and smart way to be business smart. For more information, please visit www.businessexpertpress.com, or contact sales@businessexpertpress.com.